Victory Dance

Victory Dance

A Solution for Iraq and More Common
Sense Foreign Policy

Brandon Dodds

Southern Cross Publishing

For Brandon Clay

ISBN 978-0-578-00047-3

Illustrated cover by Susan Carolin

Maps by World Sites Atlas (sitesatlas.com)

Flag clipart on back cover by worldatlas.com

Special thanks to Betty Beardsley for her editing efforts.

Contents

Maps

Preface

Over a year ago I developed a plan that should achieve all of our goals in Iraq and allow us to withdraw our troops from the region relatively quickly. After failing to achieve contact with anyone in the Bush administration, I decided to put my ideas in book form. It is not a perfect plan and would not be easy to implement, but it would have a chance at bringing a lasting peace to the region. The current policy in Iraq is not grounded in reality and has absolutely no possibility of even short-term success. I felt obligated to try to share the plan because I felt that our failure there would be devastating to our military honor and global credibility. Defeat would also have terrible implications on the world's oil supply and could easily lead to a widespread regional war.

It is my belief that disputes between peoples and nations, while exceedingly tricky are solvable. The Clinton and Bush administrations have done very little to find permanent solutions to world impasses. They have dealt in day-to-day, knee-jerk, band-aid fixes that do not have a chance at lasting. I sat down to attempt to brainstorm an alternative policy for Iraq after repeatedly hearing from regular citizens and political leaders alike that "we will never achieve success in Iraq." The Democrats in our government apparently want us to pull out no matter what the consequences. The Bush administration is dead set on "staying the course." Neither of these approaches is worthy of the American people. Our leaders owe it to their constituents to put aside their petty differences and find solutions to difficult problems. If they stop trying to think outside the box, advocate defeat, or try to keep the status quo when it is not working, then our cause is already lost.

The United States and Great Britain certainly have the military might to defeat any conventional force in the region. They must realize that this alone is not enough to ensure success. A comprehensive, flexible, realistic approach must be employed that incorporates the history of the people involved. Cookie cutter democracy would be ideal in a utopian society, but we have no business trying to force it on an advanced civilization that is not prepared for it. It may be naive to hope that our diplomats and leaders would read this book, but if they do, I hope they at least explore some of the points I have struggled to make.

I have included sections on the Balkans and Nagorno-Karabagh because I felt that U.S. policy there has been misguided, inconsistent and hypocritical. I feel that progress could be made there with strong leadership and willingness to compromise.

The historical background provided to each conflict is not in any way intended to be a primary source. It is supplied to make the reader aware of some of the events that led to the current situations.

Part One
The Balkans

Chapter 1

A House Divided Against Itself Cannot Stand

    Timely, appropriate, neutral intervention in the former
Yugoslavia by the United States and Europe's powers certainly
could have altered the course of events that occurred there in the
1990s. Instead, sadly the world watched and reacted to what was
happening at that moment in time. No consideration was given
to why events were taking place or what the future repercussions
for such myopic intervention would bring. European and U.S.
policy from the outset had a tremendous influence on the events
that followed. The diplomats of the world reached the
conclusion that the national borders of Yugoslavia could be
discarded, but the borders of the republics and autonomous
regions were inviolable. This contradictory policy allowed
republics that did not wish remain part of Yugoslavia to secede.
It also expressly forbade the minorities of these republics to
secede. When war inevitably broke out, the Serbs were painted
as the villains because of the numerous atrocities they committed
and "their" policy of ethnic cleansing. The U.S. and their allies
then tacitly supported the cleansing of the Serbs from Croatia. I
contend that if it is wrong for Serbs to commit atrocities against
Croats and Muslims, then it is equally wrong for Croats and
Muslims to commit atrocities against Serbs. The Bosnian War
was halted with a bombing campaign and a hard-negotiated
peace deal. The U.S. deserves credit for stopping the bloodbath,
however, after the "nation" was split into two entities, the U.S.
dimwittedly insisted that the Serb half remain cobbled to the

Bosniak/Croatian half. In Kosovo, NATO attacked a sovereign nation, which was dealing with a separatist terrorist organization. The shadowy KLA was actively terrorizing Serb policeman and civilians. The Serbs brutally responded, but no more so than the Russians in Chechnya or the Turks in Kurdistan. When NATO forced the Serb troops to withdraw from the region, they failed to stop the Albanians from massacring the civilian Serbs. In both the Croatian and Kosovo conflicts, the U.S. has intervened because of Serbian atrocities. In both instances the forces we backed reciprocated the atrocities and ethnically cleansed the Serbs. This U.S. policy has left the region as polarized today as ever. The old Balkan tradition has been reinforced, if you have powerful allies, you can rid a region of an unwanted people and declare it your own. U.S. and European troops currently have to maintain troops there to prevent the resumption of hostilities. They are also clinging to policies that have very little chance of settling the unresolved issues. So the region is trapped in a holding pattern. Foreign peacekeepers expensively keep war at bay, but are doing nothing to fix what is actually broken. This situation cannot go on indefinitely and after a very brief discussion of the history of the region, some common sense solutions will be discussed.

Former Yugoslavia with High-Water Mark of Croatian and Bosnian Serbs

Chapter 2

What a Tangled Web We Weave

The tribes of the Southern Slavs began raiding and
settling in the Roman region of the Balkans in the seventh
century A.D. The Roman Empire had been divided between
Rome and Constantinople in the third century. The Croats,
who predominantly settled along the Adriatic coast, generally
became Roman Catholic Christians. The Serbs, who settled
further east and south, mostly became Eastern Orthodox
Christians. Both groups spoke the same language. The Croats
use the Latin alphabet, while the Serbs use the Cyrillic
alphabet. All the Southern Slav constituents of the former
Yugoslavia: Slovenes, Croats, Serbs, Montenegrins, and
Macedonians are very closely related. Religion in the Balkans
for centuries was more of an identifying cultural characteristic
than ethnicity.

The Serbs had been divided into smaller principalities
but were united later into a single large kingdom. They
reached their territorial peak in the mid 1300s under King
Dusan. After his death, the Serbs were weakened by the
splintering of his kingdom into different principalities.
Unfortunately for the Serbs, this coincided with the advance of
the Turks further into the Balkans. At the battle of Maritsa in
1371, the Turks crushed the Serbs. Bulgaria (another south
Slav people very closely related to the Macedonians) and
Macedonia fell under Turkish rule as a consequence of this
defeat. A more famous defeat for the Serbs occurred in 1389

on St. Vitus Day (Vidovdan), a very important holiday to the Serb Orthodox church. The battle of Kosovo Polje took place on the "field of blackbirds" in Kosovo (which at the time was an undisputedly Serbian land). Both Serbian Prince Lazar and the Turkish Sultan were killed in the battle. Neither side could claim victory, and the Turks withdrew. Losses were heavy on both sides and it was clear that the Serbs would not be able to replace their casualties as easily as the Turks could. The Christian Hungarians also began to pressure the northern Serb lands rather than stand united against the Islamic threat. The Serbs held out as long as possible, but they were finally incorporated into the Ottoman Empire in 1459. The battle of Kosovo has become a legendary and central theme in Serbian heritage. Some of their most important churches and monasteries are located in Kosovo making it a historical and religious focal point for them.

The origins of the Albanians have not been definitively established. Most historians contend that they are the descendants of the ancient Illyrians. However, some researchers believe they are settlers from other parts of Europe. The Illyrians were conquered by the Romans between the 200s B.C. and 9 A.D. The division of the Roman Empire into eastern and western halves resulted in the religious division of the Illyrians. The northern areas remaining Roman Catholic and the Southern parts gravitating to the Orthodox Church based in Constantinople. The term Albanian came into use around 1000 A.D. After the fall of the Western Roman Empire around 476 A.D., the Albanian lands were predominantly ruled by the Byzantine Empire (the eastern Roman Empire). However, raiders and invaders were constantly ravaging the region. The Goths, Huns, and Slavs all raided the area. The Serbs, Bulgarians, Venetians, and Normans also were able to conquer Albania at times as the power of the Byzantine Empire rose and fell. When the Turks invaded in the late 14th century, the Albanians resisted like all the people of the Balkans. They were defeated at the battle Savra and brought under Ottoman domination. The Albanian warrior Skanderbeg led a successful revolt that bedeviled the Turks. His resistance cemented his place as the preeminent hero of the Albanian people. He had converted to Islam when he was sent to the Ottoman capital as a hostage (a common practice required by the Turks of prominent families). He became a successful Ottoman officer but denounced Islam and fought his way back to Albania. He led a corps of soldiers, who had also mutinied from the Turkish army. From 1443 to his death in 1468, he fought courageously against the Turks. The struggle persisted for about ten years after his death, but then Albania was brought back under Ottoman rule. The fall of Constantinople in 1453 had sent shock waves throughout Christendom. The Albanians, like the Serbs, now fell under a long Turkish domination.

The Croats had come to the Balkans around the same time as the Serbs. As they settled in areas under the jurisdiction of the western half of the Roman Empire, they generally became Roman Catholic. They reached the height of their medieval power in the early 900s A.D. under the guidance of King Tomislav I. The Croats were incorporated into the Hungarian Kingdom in 1102. At the Battle of Mohacs in 1526, an Ottoman army defeated the Hungarian and Croat forces. This resulted in the partition of Hungary into three parts: Ottoman, Hapsburg, and Transylvania. Croatia was fortunate to remain in the Hapsburg Monarchy. It protected them from the Turks and also united them in a kingdom with the Slovenes. The Croatians were shielded from the Turks by the creation of a "military frontier", the Krajina. Serbs were invited into the border regions of Croatia by the Hapsburgs and given benefits to protect the kingdom from the Ottomans. The Ottomans and Hapsburgs fought for the next 138 years. The Turks actually laid siege to Vienna in 1529, but were forced to retreat after failing to achieve a quick victory. A Hapsburg victory in 1664 led to a twenty-year peace, but the Turks again invaded Austria in 1683 with a massive army. A combined Austrian, Polish, and German force defeated them at the battle of Vienna. This led to the liberation of Hungary and its incorporation into the Hapsburg Monarchy. Its rule by the Turks had left much of the country depopulated. In 1867, these lands became the Austria-Hungary Empire.

The Slavs settled the mountainous region of Montenegro and assimilated the Illyrians who lived there. The Pope recognized it as independent in the early eleventh century. It was forced to pay tribute to the Byzantine Empire and later the Bulgarian Empire. Zeta, as it was then called, was at times part of a larger united Serbian Empire. However, as the Serbs fragmented into smaller principalities, it gained its autonomy. Due to its mountainous topography and the fierceness of its people, Montenegro was able to stave off conquest by the Ottomans until 1499. The Montenegrins are Orthodox Christians and there is some debate as to whether or not they are one people with the Serbs. While they and the Serbs have not always been united in one political entity, historically the two peoples have thought of themselves as the same. This is similar to the Germans of Austria and Germany; the Arabs of Jordan, Syria, Iraq, etc; and the English in Britain, Australia, Canada, United States, and the American South.

The Bulgarians arrived in the Balkans along side their fellow Slavs. They interjected themselves into the land formerly occupied by the Thracians. They were recognized by the Byzantine Empire in 635 A.D. In the early 700s, the Bulgarians helped raise an Arab siege of Constantinople. They quickly gained influence and spread throughout the Balkans. This led to conflicts with their Slavic brothers, the Serbs and Croats, along with the Byzantium Greeks. They accepted the Orthodox faith and also adopted the Cyrillic alphabet. They were finally defeated and incorporated into the Byzantine Empire in the early 11th century. In 1185, they regained their independence, but were in constant conflict with either the Hungarians or the Byzantines. The power of the Bulgarians declined in the 14th century and it splintered into principalities. In this weakened state, they were no match for the Ottomans and were swallowed into the Turkish behemoth.

The Serbs, Albanians, Hungarians, Macedonians, Montenegrins, Greeks, and Bulgarians endured a harsh occupation under the Ottoman Empire. As Christians they were supposedly a protected people, but in reality they were anything but safe. They were brutally repressed after any uprising. The subsequent massacres depopulated huge swaths of territory in the Empire. Christians often had their children seized to fill out the ranks of Janissaries or the Ottoman bureaucracy. The children were raised as Muslims and were generally merciless to the Sultan's foes. Conversion to Islam brought rewards, prestige and the hope of upward mobility. Conversion from Islam to Christianity was met with an immediate death sentence. The Turk bureaucrats generally settled in towns, while Christian peasants populated the countryside. In contrast to the other occupied peoples of the Balkans, the majority of the Albanians converted to Islam. In contrast to the Serbs, Greeks, and Bulgarians, they did not have a strong central church. In Bosnia, which was part the Ottoman Empire as well but populated predominantly by Serbs or Croats, a significant percentage of the population did convert to Islam. After their religious conversion, the Albanians and Bosnian Muslims were quick to join in the excesses of power that the Ottomans enjoyed. There had been a preexisting enmity between the Serbs and Albanians. The vitriol for the Bosnian Muslims was intense, as they were seen as traitors to both God and country. As already mentioned, the Hapsburgs invited Serb families to settle inside the borders of Croatia. The warlike Serbs relished the task of defending Christendom from the hated Turks. In exchange for their loyalty and military service they were granted tax privileges and allowed to continue religious allegiance to the Serb Orthodox Church. They provided a buffer and fought fiercely in the Empire's armies. The Croatian Army would later expel their descendants from the Krajina in 1995. In 1689, the Hapsburgs invaded the Ottoman lands and the Serbs jubilantly rose to fight for their independence. They were defeated at Kacanik, and a massive Turkish campaign of revenge was launched. Villages were put to the torch; Serb children were rounded up for slavery while the adults and elderly were slaughtered. Patriarch Arsenije of the Serbian Orthodox Church led over 30,000 Serb families out of Kosovo to escape the massacre. To repopulate the area, the Turks encouraged the migration of the newly Islamicized Albanians. There was

18

already an Albanian presence in Kosovo prior to the Serb exodus. With the new settlers, the high Albanian birth rate, and a hostile Muslim occupying force, the Serbian nature of Kosovo was diminished. The Serbs around Belgrade were able to escape the Ottoman yoke temporarily when the Hapsburgs occupied the area for about twenty years in the early 1700s. In the late 1700s, this pattern occurred yet again with the Austrians invading and then withdrawing, leaving the Serbs to the mercy of the vengeful Turks. The Serbs were now almost in constant revolt and rose en masse when their fellow Slavs and Orthodox brethren, the Russians, went to war with the Turks in 1806. The Serbs again faced retribution when the Russians signed a peace treaty and stopped fighting. The Russians and Serbs again squared off with the Turks in 1809 with a near identical outcome. The Russians quit fighting and the Turkish punishment was terrible. Villages were again systematically burned and many who could not evade the Turkish onslaught were killed outright or sold into slavery. Things began to look up for the Balkan Christians as the Ottoman power soon began to wane noticeably. The Greeks were successful in winning a war for independence and the Serbs gained autonomy guaranteed by the Russians. The last Turkish troops left in 1867. The Serbs and Montenegrins went to war with the Ottomans to aid a Christian uprising in Bosnia (which had not gained its independence). They achieved mixed results (Montenegrin success was overshadowed by Serbian defeats) until the Russians intervened. A Russian victory and its subsequent attempt to create a greater Bulgaria spooked the great European powers. They met at the Congress of Berlin in 1878 to settle the issue diplomatically. The Serb and Montenegrin territory was expanded and their independence was recognized. However, they were horrified when Bosnia was awarded to the Austria-Hungary Empire. The Serbs were the largest ethnic group in Bosnia at the time representing 42.9% of the population (they would continue to be the most populous of ethnic groups there until the 1960s). The Serbian kingdom pursued an unsuccessful war against the Bulgarians in 1886. In

1889, the Serbs, Montenegrins, and even the Croats celebrated the 500th anniversary of the fateful Battle of Kosovo. The next major Balkan bloodletting occurred in 1912. King Nicholas of Montenegro declared war on the Turks. A Turkish army was assembled in Macedonia to resist the Montenegrin thrust towards the stronghold of Shkoder. The Serbs, Bulgarians, and Greeks all launched preplanned invasions into the remaining European holdings of the Ottoman Empire (Macedonia, Kosovo, Thrace, and Albania). The Christians had formed an alliance called the Balkan League and had been waiting for an opportunity to come to blows with their Islamic nemesis. By 1913, the Turks had been thrown back almost to Istanbul. The Treaty of London was imposed by the great powers to decide the spoils of war. Albania was recognized as independent. The Serbs and Montenegrins finally gained control over the Sandzak. This strategic region separated them and had formerly been controlled by the Ottomans. It had briefly fallen under Austrian power but had recently returned to Ottoman domination. The Austrians had adopted an anti-Serbian diplomatic policy. They feared a united and powerful Serbdom would seek to collect the Croatian and Bosnian Serbs into their fold. The Serbs jubilantly also regained control of their national obsession and historical heartland, Kosovo. They ruthlessly suppressed the now majority Albanians who were not overly pleased to be "liberated." Territory in Thrace and Macedonia was disputed between the Greeks, Serbs, and Bulgarians. A second Balkan War soon erupted when the Bulgarians felt they were not getting their fair share of the conquered lands. The Serbs and Greeks fought together against the Bulgarians. When the Greeks gained the advantage, the Romanians and Turks declared war against Bulgaria as well. The Bulgarians could not hold out against its legion of enemies and lost sizeable amounts of territory. A large portion of Macedonia became "Southern Serbia," with the rest going to the Greeks.

The Balkans would not remain peaceful for long. Gavrilo Princip assassinated the crown prince of the Austria-Hungarian Empire on June 28, 1914 in Sarajevo. He was a

Bosnian Serb struggling with tuberculosis who longed for the unification of the Slavs. He claimed that the Archduke Franz Ferdinand's visit was especially insulting because it occurred on Vidovdan. He was joined in the attempt by at least five other members of Young Bosnia, an association of mostly Bosnian Serb students. The group had ties to another secret organization known as "Unification or Death" or "the Black Hand." This Serbian based group was made up mostly of military hard liners. One of its most influential members was Colonel Dragutin Dimitrijevic, who also went by his codename of Apis. Three of Princip's coconspirators were hanged while he and one other died in prison. After the assassination, the Bosnian Muslims and Croats went on a rampage. Serb businesses, property, and lives were destroyed. The Austrian authorities soon officially sanctioned these actions by organizing the mobs into military units to deal with the Serb population. Cyrillic was outlawed in Bosnia and Bosnian Serb schools were shut down. Thousands were killed or arrested. Later, when war officially broke out, conditions became even worse.

The Serbs in Bosnia were not the only ones who would pay for the Archduke's murder. After confirming Kaiser Wilhelm II of Germany's support, Austria-Hungary sent Serbia an ultimatum, which they knew could not be completely accepted. The Serbs had only forty-eight hours to respond, but they agreed to most of the terms. They refused to accept an Austria-Hungarian investigation on Serbian soil but softened the refusal with a proposal for arbitration. The German Kaiser after reviewing the Serb response felt the crisis had been defused, but Austria-Hungary went ahead and declared war on July 28, 1914. The ultimatum itself had led to mobilizations of Europe's armies. The Russians, who had begun to mobilize only on the Austrian-Hungarian front, realized that this wasn't logistically possible for them and started a general mobilization. Soon war had been declared, with Germany, Austria-Hungary and later Turkey squaring off against Great Britain, Russia, France, Serbia, and Italy. The Montenegrins stood by their Serb brothers and braced for war as well.

The Austrians were forced to divide their forces between the Italian, Russian, and Serbian fronts. They thought they would swiftly overrun the Serbs, but were initially defeated at the Battle of Cer. Another campaign led to the brief occupation of Belgrade, followed by an Austrian defeat at the Battle of Kolubara. The Serbs lost around 170,000 men and the Austrians around 230,000 men. At the end of 1914, the forces were roughly where they started, but the Serbs were in a precarious situation because they could not replace their casualties as easily as the Austrians. The Krajina Serbs of Croatia maintained their loyalty to the Austria-Hungary Empire and fought against their fellow Serbs as fiercely as they would have any enemy. The Serbian prospects were further diminished when the Germans decided to help the Austrians knock them out of the war. The Bulgarians had also been persuaded to join the Central Powers and were itching to regain their lost territories from the Second Balkan War. It was apparent that the Serbs and Montenegrins would not be able to hold out when the offensives against them began. The French and British rushed soldiers to the Greek city of Salonika, where they would stay because of Greek political turmoil. On October 7, 1915, the German/Austria-Hungarian Army began its offensive. As they drove south, the Bulgarians launched two offensives from the east on October 11. One Bulgarian thrust moved west towards Nis, and the other was launched toward Skopje, Macedonia. The Serbs were defeated in the battles of Morava, Ovche Pole, and Kosovo. Their situation was untenable, but rather than surrender they decided to retreat through Montenegro and Albania to the coast of the Adriatic Sea. The army, government, King Peter, Crown Prince Alexander, and tens of thousands of civilians set out to escape destruction. They endured hunger, cold, disease, and the hardship of a winter mountain crossing. The retreating Serbs had to move as quickly as possible to stay ahead of the armies of the Central Powers that pursued them. The Albanians of Kosovo and Albania also took the opportunity to slaughter any weak or straggling groups. Between 120,000 and 160,000 Serbs were finally evacuated by the navies of the British and

French. Most were sent to Corfu, but some were sent to islands all over the Mediterranean Sea. After being refitted and reorganized, the Serbian Army joined their Entente allies at Salonika hoping to drive north to liberate their homeland. Back in Serbia, conditions were grim for the Serbs. The Bulgarians and Austria-Hungarians maintained armies there and calling their actions brutal would be an understatement. Thousands were sent to concentration or work camps within the Austria-Hungarian Empire. The Bulgarians also began the re-Bulgarianization of Macedonia. The Serbs had been relentless in imposing Serb customs there and now the tables were turned again. The Kosovo Albanians also wreaked vengeance on their Serb neighbors. The Austria-Hungarians then invaded Montenegro and forced them to surrender on January 25, 1916. They then advanced southward into Italian occupied Albania. With the Italian defeat there, the Central Powers dominance in the Balkans was complete. The Greeks still had not definitively joined either side and were at the center of much political intrigue. The Allied troops at Salonika now began plans to turn the situation around. Romania was about to join their side and a breakout from Salonika to the north was planned. The Bulgarians launched a preemptive assault on Salonika with the help of the Germans. The Serbs and their allies not only stopped the Bulgarian advance but also counterattacked and advanced over twenty miles. The pro-German Greeks organized a surrender of part of Greek Macedonia to the Bulgarians and this treachery greatly weakened Greek sentiment toward the Central Powers. The Italians were also able to send new troops to Albania and had some success there. These results were tempered by the Russian collapse and the occupation of most of Romania by Bulgaria and Turkish troops. It was not until September of 1918 that the Serbs, French, Greeks, Czechs, and British decided the issue in the Balkans with the decisive victory at the Battle of Dobro Pole. The Bulgarians sued for peace and the Franco-Serb Army liberated Serbia. The regions' borders were about to be dramatically altered by the following treaties and political events.

On December 1, 1918, the new Kingdom of Serbs, Croats, and Slovenes was formed. King Peter I of Serbia nominally led the kingdom, but he had turned power over to his son Alexander as Prince Regent after the Balkan Wars. It was made up of Serbia and Montenegro (which had merged a short while earlier), Macedonia, and the southern Slavic lands of the former Austria-Hungary Empire (Croatia, Bosnia, and Slovenia). Union with Serbia had been favored in Montenegro, but it was not carried out in a popular fashion. King Nicholas I of Montenegro was deposed and his domain just incorporated into the Serbian kingdom. This was made possible by the presence of Serbian troops who were present following the ouster of the Austrians. Resentment was also present in Croatia, as it soon became apparent that the new kingdom was more an extension of Serbian control than a kingdom of Slavic equals. In Kosovo, the Albanians predictably revolted, and the now ingrained pattern of Balkan reprisals ensued. Albanians were massacred and as they continued to resist Serb control, they were brutally repressed. The Slovenes benefited from the new kingdom. The Serbs had no historic claims to their lands so they were able to achieve more administrative autonomy than the other Slavs. On June 28, 1921, the Vidovdan Constitution was ratified and the new national government was in place. On January 26, 1929, King Alexander I, who assumed the throne when King Peter died in 1921, dissolved the constitution and changed the name of the nation to the Kingdom of Yugoslavia. He ruled as an absolute monarch until his 1934 assassination in France. He was shot by a pro-Bulgarian, Macedonian. His son was crowned as King Peter II, but Prince Paul, a royal cousin, was appointed regent because Peter was a minor. Internal strife continued as both the Serbs and Croats wanted to add to their internal territories and carve up Bosnia.

Warfare and intrigue surrounded the nervous nation in the very late 1930s and early 1940s. Adolph Hitler's Germany and Benito Mussolini's Italy had joined forces and looked to dominate Europe. They helped Francisco Franco install a fascist dictatorship in Spain. Germany merged with Austria, absorbed Czechoslovakia, and overran Poland, Belgium, and France. Italy had occupied Albania and invaded Greece. They floundered in Greece, but the Germans soon dispatched troops there to finish the conquest. The nations of Hungary, Romania, and Bulgaria had agreed to the Axis Tripartite Pact with Germany and Italy. Russia had also signed a non-aggression pact with Germany, and the United States was technically neutral. Only Great Britain stood against the seemingly unstoppable Germans. No one felt that the British could help Yugoslavia in any meaningful way if the Germans invaded. Hitler was placing enormous pressure on the Yugoslav government and it was understood that if they did not join the Tripartite Pact they would be invaded and divided. Prince Paul stalled for months and negotiated a deal that Yugoslavia could sign and still remain effectively neutral. They would not have to support the German war effort, their borders were guaranteed, and Axis troops did not gain free access across the nation. Under those terms Prince Paul agreed to the Tripartite Pact on March 25, 1941. Although it seemed like the only reasonable choice given the circumstances, demonstrations broke out against it in Belgrade. The Serbs and Germans had been enemies for generations and the treaty was deeply unpopular. Two days later a coup replaced the regency with King Peter II. Quickly realizing that rejecting the Pact would mean annihilation, the new government sent word to Hitler that they would adhere to it. The damage had been done, however. Hitler was enraged and ordered the conquest of Yugoslavia with inexorable severity. The ensuing fight was certainly not a clash of equals. The Germans, supported by the Italians, Hungarians, and Bulgarians quickly overran the nation. Even for the Balkans, the following events were horrific.

Yugoslavia was quickly divided. Italy received large chunks of the Dalmatian coast. Italy combined Kosovo and Albania into a Greater Italian Albania. Italy also occupied Montenegro, and Germany occupied the remains of Serbia. Slovenia was divided between the Germans and Italians. Bulgaria received Macedonia. Hungary also received a large concession of land along its border. The Croats were rewarded with the Independent State of Croatia or the NDH. Ante Pavelic was installed as a German puppet. His fascist Ustasa regime declared that Serbs, Jews, and Gypsies were enemies of the state. Their 'checkerboard' symbol became as infamous in the Balkans as the NAZI swastika. The NDH was divided into German (east) and Italian (west) zones. It included all of Bosnia and Herzegovina. Serbs comprised about a third of the population of the NDH. Cyrillic was quickly banned and over 100,000 Serbs were forced to convert to Catholicism. Hundreds of thousands were expelled into rump Serbia. Mimicking their NAZI patrons, the Ustasas also set up death camps where civilians were slaughtered by the thousands. Massacres were widespread and merciless. The Ustasas, Germans, and Italians all recruited from the Muslim populations to augment their troops. They were generally more than willing to repay the Serbs for decades of domination. These outrages were guaranteed to provoke a resistance movement. Two major resistance groups formed. The Chetniks, under the leadership of Colonel Draza Mihailovic were mainly comprised of royalist Serbs. The Partisans were communist soldiers led by Josip Broz, or Tito, as he was known. The Partisans were able to recruit from Muslims, Croats, Serbs, and Slovenes. This allowed them to enjoy a wider base of support. The former nation spiraled into a confusing melee. The Partisans and Chetniks fought the Ustasas, Germans, Italians, Albanians, Muslims, and each other. They did not just attack military targets, but responded in kind when their villages were burned. Brutal German reprisals from acts of sabotage and ambushes caused Mihailovic to question attacking the Germans directly. German policy was to kill 100 Slavs for every German killed. In October 1941, they executed 5,000 civilians to try to quell the rising violence. While Mihailovic tried to gather his resources and concentrate his attacks on Ustasas and Partisans, Tito felt that the harsh German response to his attacks would draw more troops to him in the long run. Both groups held talks with the Germans to explore truces to fight the other. The Italians were more sympathetic to the Serbs and in some cases protected the civilian population and monasteries. In Kosovo, the Albanians delighted in burning villages, killing, and expelling Serbs wherever possible. The Germans were able to raise two SS divisions in Yugoslavia: the 21st Waffen Mountain "Skanderbeg" Division from the Kosovo Albanians, and the 13th Waffen Mountain "Handzar" Division from Bosnian /Sandzak Muslims and Croatians. These units proved much more adept at rape, pillage, murder, arson, and ethnic cleansing than combat. The Partisans and the Soviet Red Army liberated Belgrade on October 20, 1944, and the NDH collapsed in 1945. This finally ended the guerrilla war, but more ethnic violence was in store for the beleaguered nation. Tito and the Partisans were more than ready to fill the power vacuum that resulted from the German defeat. The British had supplied them with arms exclusively after concluding that they were more effective at fighting the Germans than the Chetniks. As the Partisans gained strength, the Chetniks' power waned. When the Partisans helped the Russians liberate Belgrade, they clearly were in a position to determine Yugoslavia's future.

The casualty figures from the war are a source of great debate. The massive number of refugees that were forced to flee the fighting further clouds them. At least 1,000,000 people died and more than half of them were Serbs. The Croat's bloody attempt to eliminate the Serbs from Croatia in the 1940s would play into the hands of Serb nationalists in the 1990s. The misery continued immediately following the war as the Partisans rounded up and massacred the Chetniks and Ustasas. They were also brutal in reestablishing control of Kosovo. Ethnic Germans were expelled to Germany or Austria. Tito established a "federal" communist Yugoslavia comprised of six republics: Serbia, Croatia, Slovenia, Bosnia-Herzegovina, Macedonia, and Montenegro. Each republic theoretically had the right to secede, but this was an unthinkable option under the heavy-handed communist regime. Tito was half Croat and half Slovene and was usually able to effectively head off ethnic crises. Immediately following the war any question of his authority was usually met with immediate execution. He later weakened the Serb Republic by instituting two autonomous regions within it: Kosovo, which was predominately Albanian, and Vojvodina, which had a sizeable Hungarian minority. While the minorities in Serbia were given autonomy, the Serb minorities in Croatia were not. The power of the Serbs was further diminished by being separated from Montenegro and by losing Macedonia. They were still in control of Bosnia because they made up the largest percentage of the Bosnian population. The Croat and Muslim wartime collaborators had tried to alter this fact, but the resistance of the Chetniks and Partisans had thwarted the attempt. Yugoslavia was held together for decades by the personality of Tito. He split with Moscow and steered the nation to neutrality during the cold war. His death in 1980 and the collapse of the Soviet Union a few years later set the stage for the ethnic groups in Yugoslavia to settle old scores once again.

In an effort to hold the nation together after Tito's death, a system was installed to rotate the presidency among the six republics and the two autonomous regions. As the power of the communists decreased, ethnic tension increased. Old wounds that had been dormant were reopened. Tensions between the Kosovo Albanians and Serbs were boiling over and the Croats, Slovenes, Macedonians, and Bosnian Muslims did not want to be involved. After Slobodan Milosevic went to Kosovo in 1987, Yugoslavia would never be the same. He was the protégé of the Serbian president, Ivan Stambolic. He had been sent to Kosovo to placate the Serb minority. They were increasingly being forced to leave the province by both active intimidation by the Kosovo Albanians and lack of opportunity in a Kosovo Albanian dominated region. The Serb population there had fallen to less than 13%. At a gathering of Kosovo Serbs at Kosovo Polje, he famously told them "No one should dare to beat you."[1] This propelled him to superstardom amongst the Serbs across Yugoslavia. He used his newfound popularity to gain the presidency of Serbia. He abolished the autonomy of Kosovo and Vojvodina. He also forced the replacement of the president of Montenegro with one of his allies. As successful as he was at rising to power, the Serbs could not have chosen a worse leader. Milosevic was an opportunist; he made decisions on a short-term basis with no regard for the long-term consequences. Worst of all, he was more than willing to sell out those, whom he had championed, just to remain in power. His willingness to make promises with no inclination of keeping them rapidly wore thin with the world powers when war came.

Not surprisingly the Slovenes and Croats were the first to begin the process of secession. In the elections of 1990, they swept the communists from power there and elected nationalist leaders. Bosnia, Serbia, and Montenegro were trying to keep the nation together while Macedonia was patiently watching the situation unfold. The Bosnians had the most to lose with a breakup of the nation because there were no Bosnians. There were Bosnian Serbs, Bosnian Muslims, and Bosnian Croats, but no distinct consciousness of being a Bosnian. The Muslims had overtaken the Serbs as the most populous ethnic group there in the early 1970s. They made up approximately 44% of the population of Bosnia, with the Serbs comprising roughly 31% and the Croats roughly 17%. There were some areas of Bosnia that were predominantly one ethnic group or another. However, the ethnic majority areas were not necessarily congruous and usually in each area one could find villages of the other ethnic groups. Any dismemberment of Bosnia would not be pretty. Bosnia's new leader was Alija Izetbegovic, who was a Bosnian Muslim. He went on record as preferring that Bosnia stay within a loose confederation of Yugoslavia but if Croatia and Slovenia seceded, Bosnia would be forced to secede as well. Slovenia declared its independence from Yugoslavia on June 25, 1991. The Croats also voted for independence, but were persuaded by the European Commission to freeze independence for three months. The Serbs had no historical or territorial issues with the Slovenes and were willing to let them go in relative peace. The Yugoslav government was basically dysfunctional by that time and the JNA, the Yugoslav army, tried briefly, half-heartedly, and unsuccessfully to reestablish federal control there. After a ten-day skirmish that the Slovenes dominated, Slovenia achieved de facto independence. The Croat and Slovene

29

soldiers in the JNA had refused to fight in the conflict and deserted to their respective homes. The Croatian president was Franjo Tudjman. His nationalist rhetoric did little to calm the Serbs in Croatia. He had the constitution rewritten in order to eliminate some of its language that included the Serbs. More ominously, the Croats adopted a flag with the infamous checkerboard on it. Brazenly and clearly intended to intimidate, German flags were also being displayed outside Croatian homes and businesses. The Serbs made up around 12% of the Croatian population and had lived there for over 450 years. They had fresh memories of the genocide of the 1940s. When Milosevic and the Serb dominated JNA began secretly arming the Krajina Serbs, there was little internal debate on whether or not it was the right decision. Especially in rural villages, the Serbs of Croatia felt they had little choice but to protect themselves. On September 30, 1990, the Krajina Serbs declared their autonomy from Croatia hoping to remain a part of Yugoslavia. The Croats responded by replacing Serbs who held government jobs. Serbs began erecting roadblocks around their villages and expelling Croats. When Tudjman ordered in Croatian troops to enforce authority, open warfare broke out in Croatia. The Serbs declared their territories to be the Republic of Serbian Krajina (RSK). The JNA intervened and secured Eastern Slavonia after the brutal siege of Vukovar. The Serbs were initially successful in Western Slavonia as well. However, a Croat counteroffensive was very successful and regained the northern half in December of 1991. The RSK forces and the JNA also secured the predominately Serb region surrounding Knin and the Kordun region. A ceasefire was signed on January 2, 1992, and left the Serbs in control of about 30% of Croatia. They had not achieved a defeat of the Croatian military; they had simply established control in areas that were predominately Serb. With the cease-fire, the JNA was forced to withdraw and United Nations monitors were placed between the warring parties. With an effective and forceful policy, the international community might very well have prevented the war in Croatia and Bosnia. The European Community had originally advocated a wise policy that

Slovenian and Croatian independence could only be recognized after a political settlement of the outstanding issues at hand. This would not have affected Slovenia tremendously, but if the Croats and Serbs had been forced to negotiate rather than go to war, thousands of lives would have been saved. Germany however, had been overtly advocating EC recognition of Slovenia and Croatia. This obviously was no shock to the Serbs because of the historical Germanic/Croat ties, but it did embolden the Croats. They knew they would gain recognition and saw absolutely no need to include protections for their minorities or negotiate with them. Germany finally announced in December of 1991, that they would unilaterally recognize the two states with or without EC support. This action not only went against common sense, but against international law. The EC followed suit and announced that they would recognize the republics that wanted independence provided they agreed to a peace process laid out by the EC. The EC refused to recognize any representation of the Bosnian Serbs, Bosnian Croats, Croatian
Serbs, or Kosovo Albanians. They decided that the republic borders of the former Yugoslavia should not be changed. This left a double standard that implied that Croatia should not have to live in a nation dominated by Serbia, but Croatian Serbs could be forced to live in a hostile Croatia. As the Croatian war sputtered to a respite, a new bloodbath was about to unfold in its neighbor to the southeast.

The UN had imposed an arms embargo on Yugoslavia in hopes of limiting the amount of weaponry available to the belligerents. This placed the Bosnian Muslims at a disadvantage when hostilities ensued. The Bosnian Serbs would be supplied by the JNA and Serbia; the Bosnian Croats would be supplied by Croatia. When Bosnian president Izetbegovic made his intentions of steering Bosnia toward independence clear, the Serbs acted. Under the political leadership of Radovan Karadzic, they declared independence from Bosnia and announced the intention to remain within Yugoslavia. This entity eventually came to be known as the Republika Srpska (RS). Its military leader was Ratko Mladic.

The JNA had armed the Bosnian Serbs well and all Bosnian Serbs in the JNA had been stationed there in preparation for war. Initially it was a one-sided fight. The Serbs were better equipped and had the initiative. They were aided by the JNA and by Serbian militia units from Bosnia and Serbia. These units were extremely violent and relished their roles in bringing destruction upon their enemies. Some dressed and wore their beards in the old Chetnik style. One militia unit from Serbia was Arkan's Tigers. They quickly gained a reputation for rape, pillage and murder. The Muslims forces also committed numerous atrocities in areas where they had the upper hand. The media quickly began to portray the Serbs as bloodthirsty and evil. Their actions were certainly inexcusable, but to portray them as lone monsters while the Muslims and Croats were committing the same atrocities was not an accurate assessment. Wars had been fought in the same manner in the Balkans for over 700 years. The Turks, Bulgarians, Germans, Austrians, Hungarians, Greeks, Romanians, Serbs, Croats, and Albanians had all waged war by burning villages, killing civilians and raping. A major difference in past Balkan wars and the wars in the 1990s was that even up to World War II women and children were slaughtered along with the men. For the most part, in the Balkan conflicts of the 90s, women and children were not executed although the women were often raped. The Muslims were very media savvy and played up any atrocity committed against them. The Serbs, surprisingly, severely limited media access even when they were on the receiving end of war crimes. The Serbs did commit the lion's share of atrocities during the Balkan wars in the 1990s. There is no excusing their behavior. However, their enemies behaved in the same way wherever they could. The Serbs had several infamous prisons in which people were tortured, beaten, and murdered. The Croats and Muslims responded with nightmare prisons of their own. The fact that all sides were conducting themselves abysmally does not make any of these actions right; it is simply the way things were.

The Serbs were able to gain control over about 70% of Bosnia that was mainly composed of areas where they had made up the prewar majority. The exception being eastern Bosnia, which had a prewar Muslim majority, but the Serbs ethnically cleansed for inclusion in the RS. The Serb territory resembled a tilted horseshoe with the Bosnian/Croat territory in the middle. The Bihac pocket was able to hold out in an area between the RSK and the RS. In that isolated pocket, there was a miniature Muslim civil war between forces loyal to Fikret Abdic, a local charismatic businessman, and forces loyal to the Bosnian government in Sarajevo. The Croats in central Bosnia and in Western Herzegovina fought against the Serbs and at times against the Muslims. They established the Croatian Community of Herzeg-Bosnia. They too committed atrocities and had atrocities committed against them. The front lines were fairly stable from 1992 to 1994. The JNA officially left Bosnia in 1992, but they left their weapons for the Bosnian Serb army and kept paying the officers' salaries that stayed to fight. The Serbs had enough artillery and good enough defensive positions to hold their territory. The Muslims had a large advantage in infantry manpower. This was augmented by Islamic mujahedin, warriors who flocked to Bosnia to fight the Christians. The Serbs received smaller numbers of volunteers from Greece, Russia, and Bulgaria. Territory did shift hands in central Bosnia as the Muslims slowly gained ground against the Croats. Sometimes the Serbs allied themselves locally with the Croats and sometimes they allied with the Muslims. Sometimes the Croats and Muslims joined forces against the Serbs. The Serbs had failed early in the war to capture Sarajevo in a frontal assault, so they settled into a siege around the beautiful city. Serb artillery and snipers would make life miserable for its inhabitants and further alienate world opinion in the process. The hapless UN went on to designate safe havens for the Muslims. However, they failed to adequately protect these havens, provide maps to delineate their borders, or to disarm the military forces in them. Bihac, Sarajevo, Gorazde, Srebrenica, Zepa, and Tuzla were declared "safe." The UN sent troops in under the name of United Nations Protection Force (UNPROFOR) to protect the Sarajevo airport and later to assist in humanitarian relief and refugee protection.

Several peace plans, the most famous being the Vance-Owen Plan, were proposed but proved unacceptable to the warring parties. The Muslims wanted the international community to help them defeat the Serbs and gain control of all of Bosnia, and the Serbs did not want to give back any of the territory they controlled. The United States policy only aggravated the situation. They held out hope of helping the Muslims by advocating a "lift and strike" policy. President Clinton had campaigned for this more forceful action in Bosnia and his Secretary of State Warren Christopher attempted to implement it. The Americans wanted to lift the arms embargo against the Muslims and use air strikes to help defeat the Serbs. The UN nations with troops on the ground correctly assumed that this policy would make them belligerents in a civil war and leave them vulnerable to attack. The U.S. policy also emboldened the Muslims and made it impossible to negotiate with them. If the concessions they were demanding were met, they simply demanded further concessions. It was very ill advised to pick a side in a three-way civil war that had no national security implications. With no regard for the history of the region or the Croat/Muslim attempted genocide of the Serbs in World War II, the U.S. settled on a policy that the Serbs were bad and deserved to lose. The actual arms embargo was a complete farce. Islamic countries were supplying large quantities of military equipment to Bosnia through Croatia. It has also been a badly kept secret that U.S. planes were involved in this clandestine effort. The U.S. was also busy leaning on the Croats and Muslims to stop fighting each other and team up against the Serbs. In Croatia, the Americans and Germans were hard at work transforming the Croatian Army into a modern fighting force. The Croats enlisted the help of Military Professional Resources Incorporated; a firm tied to the U.S. Defense Department and made up of "retired" U.S. officers. They not only provided extensive training, but they allegedly assisted in the development of the tactical assault plan that would eventually overwhelm the RSK. When a presumably Serb shell caused massive casualties in a Sarajevo marketplace, the Serbs were forced, under the threat of NATO air strikes, to pull back their heavy weapons from around the city. Russia could have been more forceful in protecting their traditional ally, but they were at a low point in power and prestige. They also became exasperated by Milosevic's untrustworthiness. They did join a U.S. led Contact Group in an effort to exert some influence on the unfolding events. The Muslims were inexplicably able to draw NATO into conducting air strikes against the Serbs because of the safe haven policy. They launched offensives against the Serbs from the safe havens of Gorazde and Bihac. When the Serbs counterattacked, NATO hit them with air strikes. This double standard left the Serbs with no illusions concerning NATO's impartiality. Former U.S. President Jimmy Carter embarrassed the Clinton diplomatic team by traveling to Bosnia and securing a cease-fire. In recent years he had tried to redeem his horrific foreign policy legacy while in office by interjecting his personal diplomacy in world crises. His truce lasted until the Muslims launched an offensive against the Serbs, violating the terms of the agreement. The Serbs were able to launch assaults in 1995 and take the safe areas of Srebrenica and Zepa. A Dutch UN force was forced to impotently stand by while as many as 8,000 Muslim men were executed by the Serbs in Srebrenica. General Mladic was present at the battlefield and this solidified his infamous reputation for waging total war. It was also the last straw for any international sympathy, with the exception of the Slavic and Orthodox nations. The fall of the two safe havens did rectify the issue of how to include them in Bosnian territory in the event of partition. The U.S. was able to persuade the Croats and Muslims to put aside their differences and once again fight the Serbs in a coordinated effort. The UN monitors stood aside and let the Croatian army launch lightning attacks that overran Western Slavonia and the Krajina region in the summer of 1995. Over 200,000 Serbs were chased from their homeland as the Croats burned villages and murdered elderly Serbs who were unable to escape. The U.S. had given Tudjman what he interpreted as a "green light" for the offensive by only giving him a very mild warning not to proceed. The scenes of Serbs fleeing the ethnic cleansing of their enemies did not alter the media's view or the American diplomatic mantra that the Serb's were the "bad guys" and "got what was coming to them." The U.S. ambassador to the U.N., Madeleine Albright, increased her rhetoric for the world to take a harder line with the Serbs. To top off the Krajina Serbs misery at losing everything they had, they had to come to grips with the fact that they were sold out by Milosevic. The RSK troops were not ordered to resist and the JNA had made it clear that they would not intervene to help.

The stage was now set for a power shift in Bosnia as well. The Croatian military intervened directly and launched a co-offensive with the Muslims from the west that captured much of northwest Bosnia. NATO facilitated their assault by launching massive air strikes on Serb defenses, command and control, and communications. The air assault was in response to another marketplace shelling. By the time the Serbs were able to stop the advance, they held only around 49% of Bosnia. Not coincidently this was the figure that the U.S. insisted that they could have, leaving the Muslim/Croats 51%. The Bosnian Serbs were now demoralized and agreed to ceding their negotiating interests to Milosevic. The warring parties' representatives were secluded on the Wright-Patterson Air Force Base near Dayton, Ohio to hammer out a peace plan. It would come to be known as the Dayton Agreement. Richard Holbrooke was masterful in forcing concessions from each side in order to reach a final agreement. This left Bosnia as one nation made up of two republics, the RS and the Federation of Bosnia Herzegovina (FBiH). The Serbs gave up land around Sarajevo, and the Croats were forced to give back some of their late gains in northwest Bosnia. Each side retained its own military and the government structure prevented one side from dominating the other. The agreement and peace was enforced by 60,000 NATO troops known as IFOR. It certainly achieved the immediate end of hostilities, but even the casual student of the Balkans realizes that this is not a permanent solution.

Bosnia with Current Political Boundaries and
Demographics

The Kosovo Albanians shockingly and admirably pursued a policy of nonviolent resistance during the wars in Croatia and Bosnia. Following their loss of autonomy, many Albanians were removed from their government jobs. The police force and education system was also purged of Albanians. On July 2, 1990, a Kosovo Albanian parliament voted to secede from Serbia and remain a part of Yugoslavia. Later, the parliament, which was not recognized by Serbian authorities, organized a referendum for independence. After it was overwhelmingly supported in a popular vote, the parliament voted on October 19, 1991, for complete independence of the Republic of Kosova. Ibrahim Rugova was elected president of the new "nation" by his colleagues in the preeminent political force in existence there at the time, the LDK. A supplemental health and educational system was set up by the LDK. Serb refugees from Croatia and Bosnia were settled in Kosovo, and land laws were changed to make it hard for Albanians to buy Serbian land. The Serbian police was also heavy handed in dealing with the Kosovo Albanian population. Their aim seemed to be to make the Albanians too afraid to rise in revolt. The Albanians endured the police state and boycotted the Yugoslav elections. The situation seemed stable until the KLA (Kosovo Liberation Army) emerged as a viable but very small resistance group. It had been formed from several splintered Kosovo Albanian groups and was very secretive. This group launched a campaign targeting Serb policeman and civilians, as well as Albanians who were deemed as collaborators. The Serb police responded by burning villages and harsh repression. The Serbs often responded brutally against innocent local Albanians who were targeted when the KLA used hit and run tactics. "President" Rugova denied the existence of the KLA for years. He claimed that the Serbs were attacking their own people as an excuse to attack Albanian villages. Events began to change rapidly after the government of Albania collapsed in 1997. The Albanian people had invested heavily in pyramid schemes. When these schemes inevitably ran their courses and crashed, a financial meltdown ensued. The Albanian people took to the streets and the army deserted. There was effectively no viable government in Albania; it became a failed state. Government opposition factions carved out political fiefdoms, but often the real power lay with organized crime syndicates. This had a tremendous effect on Kosovo. The Serbs, though extreme in their methods, had been very effective in rooting out weapon caches and capturing violent resistance cells. When Albania collapsed, the government military arsenals were looted and the region was literally flooded with Kalashnikov automatic rifles. The KLA was able to arm larger units and tried to seize swaths of territory. Like clockwork, the Serbs launched exaggerated responses and civilian casualties mounted. Madeleine Albright, who was now President Clinton's Secretary of State, began warning the Serbs that Kosovo was not just their internal affair. At the same time, most Western governments considered the KLA a terrorist organization due to their activities. After diplomatic intervention from the American State Department ground to a halt, Richard Holbrooke was asked by the Albanians to intervene. Although Albright was furious, she relented and Holbrooke returned from the private sector to attempt to mediate between the two sides. During this time, the Serb military allowed the KLA to seize about one fourth of Kosovo and remained on the defensive. The KLA's ranks increased exponentially, and they achieved almost universal support from the Kosovo Albanian population. Of course the Serbs in Albanian controlled regions did not share their enemies' enthusiasm. They were often driven from their homes and many executions were documented. This was usually ignored in the Western media and governments. The conflict was portrayed as a human rights tragedy. The Serbs were again accused of waging another "genocidal" campaign. An objective assessment would have been that the two combatants were fighting another struggle in an ongoing quest for control of the province. This conflict dated back over 600 years, and was simply an attempt by both sides to gain control of the same land. That the Serbs now made up only about 10% Kosovo's population did not diminish Yugoslavia's sovereign rights there. Traveling between Kosovo and Belgrade,

Holbrooke and Christopher Hill, Ambassador to Macedonia, were able to arrange a meeting between Rugova and Milosevic. However, the talks led nowhere and undermined Rugova's credibility with his people. An unplanned picture of some KLA soldiers and Holbrooke greatly encouraged the Kosovo Albanians and caused consternation among Serbs. In May of 1998, the Serbs finally launched limited counteroffensives against the Albanians. The KLA soldiers usually faded away as the Serbs advanced, only to reappear and seize more territory elsewhere. Internally hundreds of thousands of refugees were on the move in the province. The KLA continued their campaign of terrorizing Serb civilians and also destroyed historic Serb Orthodox monasteries. The Serbs continued to respond with greater atrocities of their own, and this only increased their "bad guy" stereotype. Milosevic had been uncharacteristically holding the Serb military back. Most of the fighting had been done by Interior Ministry and police forces. The Kosovo Serbs were desperate for their army to intervene as the KLA got stronger and controlled more territory. On October 8, 1998, a meeting took place in London's Heathrow airport that was to seal the fate of the Kosovo Serbs. Albright and Holbrooke met with officials and foreign ministers from Austria, France, Russia, Britain, and Germany. The French diplomat wanted to get U.N. Security Council approval to act in Kosovo. The Russian Foreign Minister, Igor Ivanov, announced that if the issue was taken to the U.N., the Russians would veto it. However, he also let the assembled diplomats know that if they did not take the issue before the U.N. and handled it themselves, that the Russians would just denounce them. The Russians were not the Cold War power they once were and their military was overstretched and inadequately funded. However, their capitulation and surrender of any influence on Balkan policy left the Serbs hung out to dry. If they had taken a firm stand, the West would have had to take notice. As it was, Holbrooke and Albright received a green light to intercede however they saw fit. Secretary Albright had already gone on record as advocating that NATO had "the legitimacy to stop a catastrophe."[2] Holbrooke was able to force Milosevic, under the threat of NATO air strikes, to agree to a draw down of his troop levels to prewar numbers, to allow international monitors, and to allow NATO overflights to monitor the province. A NATO force also began assembly in Macedonia in order to be prepared to rescue the monitors if they were in danger. The Serbs began to comply with the agreement, but the KLA had not been party to the agreement and as the Serb troops were withdrawn, the KLA advanced. The Kosovo Albanians were able to return to their homes, and the KLA was able to reorganize. The Serbs felt like they had been tricked, but they had no recourse. To say that the U.S. and NATO held an overwhelming superiority in military capability compared to the Serbs would be a gross understatement. The Russians had made it clear that they would not stand in the way so the Serbs did what they had to do given the situation. They sent their military back into Kosovo. If they had not, the KLA would have continued to retake territory and cleanse the Serbs; they would lose Kosovo. For all the promises he had broken and lies he had told, Milosevic broke this agreement out of absolute necessity. He had been forced (with his nation at gunpoint) to accept a deal while his enemies could act as they pleased. Open warfare did not resume during this time, but small violent conflicts repeatedly took place. The monitors were in danger and were always trying to implement cease-fires and get hostages released. After the Yugoslav army ambushed a KLA patrol returning from Albania, the Kosovo Albanians stepped up their campaign against Serb civilians. Serb café patrons were shot or bombed in several acts of terrorism. After a KLA attack on a police patrol, the Serbs had had enough and attacked the village of Racak. Nine KLA soldiers were killed along with approximately 45 civilians.

The international response was a peace conference in Rambouillet, France. The idea was to sequester the two sides Dayton style and hammer out an agreement that would then be enforced. This concept was sound in theory, but its actual implementation was a joke. Under threats from NATO the Serbs had to come to the table and the KLA also begrudgedly decided to send a diplomatic team. They balked on the opening day of the conference amid threats that the Serbs would have them arrested upon their arrival. However, after assurances of their safety, they were flown in. The Kosovo Albanian team totaled 16 diplomats who represented several factions. They were in fact splintered amongst themselves. Rugova and his lieutenants came to represent the LDK. The KLA also was well represented. Minor parties also contributed delegates, along with prominent politicians. The Serbs sent lawyers and low-level diplomats, as well as token representatives of some of Kosovo's other minorities. The Albanians were also supplied with lawyers to help them make sense of the legal wrangling. The sides were presented some "non-negotiable principles" which stated that Yugoslavia's integrity would be not compromised and that any agreement would be only a three-year interim agreement. The conference was scheduled to end after one week, but as it drew to a close, the sides were still far apart. The Albanians wanted a promise of eventual independence, and the Serbs wanted to avoid a NATO occupation force. Albright intervened personally to persuade the Albanians to sign a negotiated document. Neither they nor the Serbs had been willing to sign the document because of its failure to promise a referendum for independence and its inclusion of a NATO occupying force. She pointed out that if the Albanians signed the document and the Serbs did not, that NATO would bomb the Serbs. Even though the logical conclusion to this reasoning would be that NATO would occupy Kosovo and the Albanians would achieve their goals, they hesitated to sign. The KLA had promised to execute anyone who signed a document that did not promise independence, and this threat carried serious weight with the delegation. The American lawyers and Albright tried to change the wording of the agreement at the last minute to suggest a referendum. This would have easily allowed the Albanians to sign. The Russians and the Contact Group blocked this change. The Albanian delegation finally compromised and agreed to sign after two weeks of consulting the Kosovo Albanian people. They also firmly believed that the document would lead to a NATO force and eventual independence of Kosovo in three years. Another meeting in Paris was scheduled for a few weeks later where the two sides would decide whether or not to agree. On March 18, 1999, in Paris, the Kosovo Albanians, British, and Americans signed the Rambouillet Accords. The Serbs and the Russians refused. The Serb military, in anticipation of the inevitable NATO bombing, began offensives in an attempt to crush the KLA. The NATO bombing campaign began on March 24, 1999.

The air campaign against Serbia and Montenegro involved over 1,000 NATO aircraft. The planes were based in mainly Italy and on aircraft carriers in the Adriatic Ocean. Tomahawk missiles were also used extensively from warships and submarines. They targeted infrastructure targets in Serbia and Montenegro, as well as military targets in Kosovo. Any dual-use (civilian-military) targets were acceptable after NATO members had approved them. Several high profile mistakes occurred including bombing an Albanian refugee convoy and the Chinese Embassy. As the bombing started, the Yugoslav army began Operation Horseshoe. Over 850,000 Albanians were expelled from Kosovo as refugees. They were packed on trains, bused out, and herded out in large convoys of vehicles and tractors. The Serbs also employed their infamous paramilitaries, some of whom had been released from prison to do the dirty work. They executed hundreds of men, robbed at will, and perpetrated thousands of rapes. This occurred against the backdrop of battles between the Yugoslav Army and the KLA as the NATO bombing campaign intensified. The Serbs were very successful in isolating and defeating the KLA. The major exception occurred on the Albanian border where the KLA was aided by Albanian artillery and direct NATO air support. The ethnic cleansing by the Serbs cemented NATO's resolve. The air strikes were not particularly effective in stopping the ethnic cleansing or demolishing the Serb military in Kosovo. They were often decoyed with fake tanks and equipment. Serb antiaircraft attempts were also largely ineffective at shooting down aircraft. They only shot down two planes, but they forced NATO to keep the planes at a higher altitude to avoid the air defenses. This directly hampered the NATO attempt to destroy small units on the ground in Kosovo. As the air campaign drug on, the possibility of a ground invasion was rumored; however, President Clinton had promised that this would not occur. This strengthened the Serb morale even though plans were developed for a NATO invasion. The Serbs had hoped to start satellite wars in Macedonia and Bosnia but were unsuccessful. Their pleas for help from their Russian "protectors" also fell on deaf ears. They hoped for Greece, as an Orthodox NATO member, to press for the discontinuation of the campaign. However, the Greeks withstood their internal overwhelming popular support of the Serbs and held the NATO line. After realizing that NATO was not going to stop the bombing, Milosevic admitted defeat on June 4, 1999. On June 10, he signed a peace agreement and the air campaign was suspended. The agreement called for the withdrawal of Yugoslav military and police from Kosovo. An 18,500-man NATO and Russian force called KFOR, advancing from Macedonia, would replace them. To the shock of international observers, as the Albanian refugees returned, they began a concerted campaign to ethnically cleanse the Serbs and Gypsies from Kosovo. They felt the Gypsies had aided the Serbs. The KLA also executed any Kosovo Albanians they felt had collaborated with the Serbs. At least 1,000 murders had been credited to their rampage. Serb villages were also torched and rapes against women were reported. Orthodox monasteries were burned and desecrated. The NATO forces were not remotely sufficient to protect Kosovo's minorities and over 250,000 Serbs and Gypsies were driven out. The KLA was able to exchange their military uniforms for police uniforms. The same international community that branded them a terrorist organization now anointed them lawmen. The KLA then launched campaigns to start ethnic Albanian insurrections in Macedonia and southern Serbia. The Serbs had been forced to withdraw three miles from their border, but after the Albanians began attacking police in this buffer zone, the Serbs were allowed to reestablish control there. A NATO ceasefire and intervention force defused the brief Macedonian Albanian and Macedonia dust up. The situation in Kosovo remains grim for Serbs; they are still continuously harassed and murdered if they leave their ethnic enclaves. The international community seems intent on allowing Kosovo's independence without regard for what's left of its minority peoples. A negotiating deadline passed in December 2007 without a compromise between Serbia and Kosovo. The Albanians saw no need to compromise on any issue because they had the backing of the United States. Although Russia tried to force further negotiations, the U.S. encouraged the Albanians to declare independence. On February 17, 2008, Kosovo's parliament declared its unilateral independence from Serbia. The next day the U.S., Great Britain, Turkey, Germany, and eight other nations recognized Kosovo as an independent nation. They did so despite China and Russia opposing the recognition as illegal in an emergency U.N. Security Council meeting. The Associated Press quoted Alejandro Wolff, the U.S. deputy ambassador to the U.N., as saying the United States is "not particularly concerned or sees no particular danger to be worried about" regarding the safety of the Kosovo Serbs.[3] The ethnic cleansing of the remaining Serbs from Kosovo is almost a foregone conclusion if the U.N. pulls its forces out. Madeleine Albright reportedly continues to count the intervention she led in Kosovo as one of her crowning achievements.

Kosovo

Chapter 3

Those Who Do Not Know History Are Doomed to Repeat It

U.S. and international intervention in the Balkan wars of the 1990s was simply not carried out in an impartial manner. As a direct result of their actions, over 500,000 Serbs were cleansed from Croatia, Bosnia, and Kosovo. This policy was carried out to stop the Serbs from ethnically cleansing the Croats, Bosnians, and Kosovo Albanians. It is unfathomable to me how a policy that condemns one side in a conflict dating back hundreds of years is justified. If the Serbs had been the only combatants committing war crimes, intervention against them could have been justified. It is now clearly understood that all sides in these conflicts were engaged in various degrees of the same activities. Engineering the defeat of the Serbs in three separate wars and allowing the atrocities against them to proceed following those wars is absolutely criminal. The Croats have not been forced to allow the repatriation of the Krajina Serbs. An uneasy peace is maintained in Bosnia by an expensive peacekeeping force. IFOR was replaced by SFOR, and the NATO troops there were reduced to 31,000 soldiers. Troop levels were later reduced to 13,000, then 7,000. The European Union took over the peacekeeping role there with around 7,000 soldiers (EUFOR). They continue to provide an uneasy peace. However, if they are withdrawn, a resumption of hostilities would more than likely not be long in forthcoming. The U.S., under its "train and equip" policy, has more than altered the balance of power in Bosnia. The Muslim/Croat army has been transformed with superb training and an influx of heavy weapons. EUFOR's main function now seems to be to protect the RS from the Bosnian Federation. The Muslims are eager to exert their control over more territory. They don't think Dayton rewarded them enough; and with their newly acquired military power, they are supremely confident.

Intervention in Kosovo flew squarely in the face of international law. Even NATO does not have the right to intervene in the sovereign affairs of a nation without United Nations approval. To claim it did so to avert a humanitarian crisis is laughable. More murders were committed in the U.S. in the year preceding NATO intervention than civilians killed in Kosovo. It should be obviously hypocritical to intervene in Kosovo where hundreds were being killed, when in Rwanda and Sudan true genocides were taking place with hundreds of thousands being killed. The Kurds in Turkey, Tibetans in China, Palestinians in the West Bank, Basque in Spain, Sahrawis in Western Sahara, Muslims in Indian Kashmir, Chechens in Russia, Armenians in Nagorno-Karabagh, and the Irish in Northern Ireland were all ethnic groups who wanted independence in the face of various degrees of oppression. To decide that the Kosovo Albanians, above all others, warranted breaking international law is not plausible. The fact is that the Serbs did not have powerful protectors and were not U.S. allies. When the Serbs tried to appeal to the International Court of Justice to stop the NATO bombing, their case was dismissed on a technicality. Yugoslavia (Serbia and Montenegro) was not a member of the U.N., so they were not eligible to appeal to the Court of Justice. Of course this did not stop a war crimes tribunal from indicting mostly Serbs from the Balkan Wars.

In Kosovo, with independence seemingly achieved, NATO is still maintaining 16,000 soldiers. Their presence is necessary for the short and long term for two reasons. First of all, they are absolutely vital to protecting the Serbs, Gypsies, and Slavic Muslims who remain there. Without military protection, their Kosovo Albanian "countrymen" would quickly drive them out. Secondly, the NATO force prevents a Serbian invasion. Throughout the long course of warfare in the Balkans, history has shown that ethnic cleansing can be reversed with ethnic cleansing. The Serbs are well versed in their history and still mourn the loss of a battle in 1389. I'm sure they will not forget their U.S. facilitated cleansing at the hands of the Albanians (or Croats for that matter). They may not strike in the near future, but to Serbs and Montenegrins, Kosovo is their heartland. It is their ancestral home, religious center, and contains their most famous battlefield. They may bide their time for decades or centuries, but as the world balance of power shifts, they will move to avenge Kosovo yet again. If Russia regains its prestige and power, and the U.S. continues its current decline, the Serbs won't have long to wait. The United States is facing rampant illegal immigration that is destroying American faith in its government as well as taxing its health and social security programs. It is also accruing massive foreign debts as its national spending skyrockets. Political correctness and militant secularism are destroying the spiritual bedrock that the nation was built on. Its international prestige is at an all time low following its post invasion failure of Iraq. Russia is also reemerging as a world power. Under the strong leadership of Vladimir Putin and his successor Dmitry Medvedev, the Russians are not floundering helplessly as they were under Boris Yeltsin. If hostilities break out again, it would be more difficult for NATO to impose its skewed brand of justice on the Balkans today.

If the status quo is maintained in the Balkans, we will see decades of continued peacekeeping efforts at a cost of billions of dollars. If peacekeepers are pulled from Kosovo, we will see the further cleansing of Serbs from their historical and religious home. If they are pulled from Bosnia, we will see a renewed war that could suck in Croatia, Serbia, Montenegro, Albania, Greece and Turkey. Proactive thinking by the American diplomats should look for true solutions not stopgap measures that freeze conflicts in time with the aid of thousands of troops. As arrogant and implausible as it may seem, lasting solutions here are not impossible. A Dayton style peace conference should be implemented. It should seek permanent solutions in Croatia, Bosnia, Kosovo, and Macedonia. All parties should be represented and have their rights respected without undue prejudice from the great powers. At no time should one side be coerced to sign treaties just to give a pretext for an invasion of another country. All sides should be forced to negotiate and should have representatives of their historical protectors present: Germans for the Croats, Russians for the Serbs, Turks for the Albanians, and Americans for the Bosnian Muslims. The Bulgarians, Albanians, Greeks, and Cypriots should also participate and perhaps the situation in Cyprus could be addressed. Several self-evident truths should be recognized and brought to fruition. The Bosnian Serbs have an absolute right to join their brethren in Serbia. They have aspired for this for centuries and have always been denied by conquerors or greater powers. If they were united with Serbia, they would not have to fear an invasion by the Bosnian Muslims. The Serbs should also receive Brcko as it is the only connection between western and eastern RS. The Bosnian Serb and Serb combined military might, would discourage further violence in Bosnia. The Serbs would also not be likely to provoke a war themselves because they are just now emerging as a world pariah and rebuilding their economy. If the Croats are not willing to allow the Krajina Serbs to return and to guarantee their rights, then the Serbs in Bosnia should be compensated. The Croats maintain control of several almost exclusively Serb populated districts and they should be transferred to the RS. If that were to happen, the Serbs would in turn need to renounce further claims against Croatia proper. Croatia should not be allowed, after cleansing the Serbs completely from Croatia, to keep more than their share of Bosnia. Even though the Croats and Muslims have powerful allies in the U.S. and Germany, all sides should be treated equally. The Serbs should receive a percentage of Kosovo. The exact percentage should be determined by the conference powers and negotiations, but anywhere from 18-25% would seem fair. The Albanians and Serbs have been fighting over this territory for over 600 years. Whoever has been in charge there, has oppressed and tried to ethnically cleanse the other. The U.S. has apparently been duped into thinking that Kosovo is simply a civil rights story. In fact it is just a very old conflict between two

50

peoples over the same land. The Kosovo Albanians should not just be handed Kosovo in its entirety, just because the Serbs were hard on them in the 1990s. That is silly, when you consider the Albanians in Kosovo were just as hard on the Serbs in the 1980s. The Serbs clearly need to maintain control of the northern districts where they make up a majority. They should also receive contiguous land to Kosovo Polje and some of their important monasteries. The Serbs, who make up the majority in some southern enclaves, would need to be relocated to the north where they could live safely. Population exchange in this day and age may sound harsh. However, it is preferable to do it voluntarily and in safety, than by burning, killing and raping people out of their homes. If the Kosovo Albanians deserve independence from the Serbs, then the Kosovo Serbs deserve independence from the Kosovo Albanians. Protection for the Roma should also be guaranteed. The Kosovo Albanians should be allowed complete independence and the ability to join Albania or have Albania join them if they wish. The northwestern Macedonian districts that are overwhelmingly Albanian should also be let go as well since lasting solutions are being sought. Bulgaria and Greece should also work out their differences with Macedonia. If Macedonia truly wants to join Bulgaria, then the international community should allow it. If they do not want to join Bulgaria, then their independence should be maintained. Greece should end its dispute of Macedonian symbols and name. With dynamic, forceful, and fair leadership, real and lasting solutions could be achieved. It would not be easy and would take compromise on all the parties' behalf, but it would be an opportunity to foster peace and cooperation in the Balkan community. The region may even one day be considered a haven for stability and prosperity.

Map of Proposed Serbia, Bosnia and Kosovo

Part Two
The Middle East

Chapter 4

Quicksand

     The Bush administration's current policy in Iraq is
tragically flawed. It represents a complete misunderstanding of
the Iraqi people and their culture. Iraq is an ancient civilization
and its inhabitants are very proud of their achievements and
religion. Modern Iraq was created from a British mandated
region in the 1920s. It is essentially inhabited by three broad
communities: the Kurds, the Sunni Arabs, and the Shiite Arabs.
     The Kurds are the largest ethnic group in the world
without their own country. They make up the majority of the
population in northern Iraq. Their numbers in Iraq have been
estimated at roughly 4,800,000. This is approximately 17 to
18% of Iraq's total population. The Kurds also inhabit a large
area of eastern Turkey, as well as, parts of Syria and Iran. They
would prefer to unite with their brethren throughout the Middle
East and form an independent Kurdistan. This puts them at
constant odds with the Turkish government, which desperately
wishes to prevent any form of independence for the Kurds. The
Turks do not want their own Kurds to have autonomy, so they
would love to see Iraq's Kurds weakened. The Kurds are
predominately Sunnis, although about ten percent are adherents
of Shi'ism. They have deep historical claims to the major oil
city of Kirkuk. Under Saddam Hussein, Sunni Arabs were
relocated to Kirkuk while Kurds were moved out. He hoped to
achieve greater Arab presence there to solidify his rule in the
important city. Since the United States defeated Iraq's

conventional armed forces and occupied the country, Kurds are returning to Kirkuk in droves. The Kurds are determined to reestablish it as part of the Kurdish autonomous region. The small Turkish minority in northern Iraq and Turkey itself would prefer Kirkuk not go completely to the Kurds. They fear that the wealth of oil deposits under the city would enrich the Kurds and allow them to amass power and military muscle. The Kurds are the one bright spot in the United States' Iraq policy. They have to date achieved a relative calm in Iraqi Kurdistan with the help of their militia, which is known as the peshmerga. It is comprised of roughly 80,000 warriors. They helped clear their region of Iraqi troops and Islamic extremists during the 2003 U.S. invasion. Generally, the Kurds have been very appreciative of the no-fly zone that the U.S had maintained over them since 1991. Although the majority of Kurds are Sunnis, they have no desire to be drawn into an Arab Sunni-Shiite civil war.

The Sunni Arabs have long dominated Iraq. They make up around 16.5% of the population with roughly 4,500,000 people. The British established a Sunni monarchy in Iraq when they granted it independence in 1932. It was overthrown in 1958, and since then power has firmly rested in the hands of Sunni strongmen. The Sunnis are distraught over the prospect of losing power in Iraq. They will defy and fight against any form of government the U.S. puts in power that does not protect their hegemony. Their insurgency against the al-Maliki government incorporates various factions. The longer the instability lasts, the more powerful al-Qaeda is becoming there. Al-Qaeda is trying to unite and radicalize all the insurgents under their umbrella to fight both the U.S. and Shiites. This has led to some infighting among the Sunnis as former Baathists and more secular minded Sunnis are resisting the predominately non-Iraqi al-Qaeda mujahedin. Even Sunnis who initially supported the coalition invasion and government have increasingly been forced to turn against it as the nation has descended into anarchy. The upper and middle classes have either fled the country or clustered in Sunni strongholds. Insurgency groups have flourished out of necessity for protection against Shiite death squads and general lawlessness. It is doubtful the Shiite led Iraqi forces, even with the help of the American military, could ever stamp out the Sunni opposition completely. Not only are they a resilient and cunning foe, they are supported by neighboring Sunni states. The Saudis, Jordanians, and Egyptians have a vested interest in seeing Sunni dominance continue. They are willing to pour resources and gunmen into the conflict there to help their co-religionists. The Saudis have hinted that they will intervene directly in the conflict when the Americans withdraw and complete chaos ensues.

The Shiite Arabs are the most numerous of Iraq's component peoples. They represent over 60% of the Iraqi population with around 17,000,000 people. They have long suffered under Sunni Arab domination and now are more than happy to turn the tables. Like the Sunni Arabs and the Kurds, they are divided into factions. One of the Shiites' most highly regarded and influential leaders is grand ayatollah Ali al-Sistani. He has been influential in brokering cease-fires between the Coalition forces and the more radical Mahdi Army that is led by Muqtada al-Sadr. Prime Minister Nuri al-Maliki is a Shiite Arab. Though they have a leadership role in the government and reconstituted armed forces, the Shiites have made it clear that they want more power. The military has been accused of aiding in the ethnic cleansing of Sunnis from predominately Shiite areas. The Shiites are also thought to favor a theocracy similar to the government of Iran. While Iran has supported the Shiite cause in Iraq, the Iranian Persians and Iraqi Shiite Arabs have always been rivals. It is widely believed that if the Coalition forces leave Iraq in its current state, the government would dissolve instantaneously. The Shiites would try to replace al-Maliki with a religious leader and crush the Sunni Arabs. The Sunnis in turn are equally confident that they can regain their preeminence through violence. The Kurds just hope to be left alone and resent Turkey's constant effort to undermine them.

It was not realistic to impose democracy upon this nation of three different peoples. Iraq and Mesopotamia are known as the Cradle of Civilization, but they have never operated under a republican system of government. The Arabs and Kurds are still fiercely loyal to tribes and chieftains; it is the way things have been done there for millennia. They are a cultured people and understandably resent having a radical system of government forced upon them. Even if Iraq were homogenous ethnically and religiously, they would instinctively resist a foreign power dictating the manner in which they are governed. Any solution should take their culture and history into account. While the American democracy has worked fine in the United States over the past one hundred and thirty years, that doesn't mean it can be imposed upon an unwilling people whose civilization predated them by thousands of years.

The Arabs also realize the long-term implications of a true democracy. Iraq does not exist in a vacuum. Shiite Iran and Syria (which is predominately Sunni, but controlled by an Alawite Shiite minority) are notorious for meddling in surrounding nations' affairs. Syria in particular has thwarted U.S. policy in Lebanon for decades. Both Iran and Syria have supported the Shiites in Iraq with their struggle against the Sunnis. They have also been major benefactors to Hamas in Gaza/West Bank and Hizbollah in Lebanon. Iraq's Sunni neighbors are also poised to enter the fray if a full-blown civil war erupts. In this violent atmosphere, each election would have life or death implications for the minority people. The only way to give democracy even a slight chance of success would have been to flood the country with occupation forces. Martial law and the security it provided may have allowed the new system to gain traction. After years of Sunni vs. Shiite violence, cooperation now is inconceivable under the current government model.

The Shiites, even with U.S. restraint, have shown themselves incapable of ruling magnanimously. The new Iraqi army is unable to conduct itself in a professional manner. It melts away when ordered to fight determined foes. It has been widely reported to collude with Shiite militias or commit crimes in its own right. The U.S. has been unable to attract the men it needed to form a reliable military corps. The Sunnis are seen as collaborators if they join. The Shiites who join are more loyal to sectarian interests. If a professional cadre of soldiers could be trained under the current system, it certainly should have been possible after four years. The men who are in the Iraqi army are simply not motivated to fight for a fleeting puppet regime.

The current troop surge in Iraq is prolonging the inevitable. It is quelling violence where the U.S. has committed large numbers of troops and letting it shift to uncontrolled regions. When U.S. soldiers leave a pacified area, it is immediately reinfiltrated by insurgents or militias. Coalition soldiers have done everything asked of them, but they cannot provide a military solution to a political problem. The current Iraqi government can only exist under the direct protection of coalition forces. It is disingenuous to suggest it has any chance of longevity.

The actual invasion has been widely discredited by both politicians and the public alike. It has been widely hypothesized that the Bush administration invaded to correct the mistake of not replacing Saddam after the first Gulf War. Some have come to believe it was all over oil, or to pay Saddam back for a failed assassination attempt on former President, George Herbert Walker Bush. In hindsight, we are now fairly confident that Iraq no longer possessed weapons of mass destruction at the time of the invasion. The evidence for a palpable link between Saddam's regime and al-Qaeda is also tenuous. While the reasons for a U.S. invasion may not look as good as they once did, the invasion itself was not the absolute blunder it is now portrayed to be. It may indeed have been carried out for the wrong reasons, but it was a move that had the potential to stabilize the region and cement our influence there. Saddam certainly led the world community to believe that he was continuing his quest for nuclear, chemical, and biological weapons. He had used chemical weapons against the Iraqi Kurds in the 1980s. Even his own people and generals thought he still had a secret unconventional weapons program. He also fought previous wars with two of his neighbors and was a general threat to the region. His continued defiance to U.N. resolutions and U.S. threats had to be addressed. The U.S. had gained a reputation for weakness in the Arab world. President Carter failed to decisively solve the Iranian hostage crisis. President Reagan abandoned Lebanon shortly after the Marine barrack bombing. The first President Bush failed to finish off Saddam in the first Gulf War. President Clinton left Somalia in chaos after the bloody battle in Mogadishu. President George W. Bush continues to stand by impotently as Sudan's Arabs butcher their African countrymen. Syria, Iran, and Iraq have all thumbed their noses repeatedly at U.S. policies. Saddam knew the U.S. possessed the finest military in the world, but he also felt America did not have the political will to fight a prolonged conflict. The Middle East viewed America as soft. A failure to address Saddam's obstinacy would have deepened this perception and left the West more vulnerable to attacks. It is easy to take a swing at a tough guy if you know he won't fight back.

The invasions of Afghanistan and Iraq could have gone a long way to turn that perception around. The war itself was not the blunder, the failure to secure the peace was. The overthrow of the Taliban using mainly air power and Afghan resistance forces should have been followed up with a massive, nationwide stabilization force and rebuilding project. Those actions could have prevented the return of personal warlord fiefdoms there and possibly allowed for the capture of Osama bin Laden. No Iraqi war should have been embarked upon until Afghanistan was viable and capable of providing its own security. Common sense dictates that a difficult job should be completed before beginning another tough task. The invasion of Iraq prevented us from providing enough troops to support the Afghan government. The amount of American and NATO troops in Afghanistan are insufficient to provide security anywhere except the area immediately surrounding Kabul. Maintaining coalition troops there certainly poses another strain on the American military, and those soldiers would certainly be helpful in patrolling Iraq. The failure to adequately provide security for post war Afghanistan was an ominous harbinger of how Iraq would be handled.

The administration has proven it did not have a plan for post war Iraq. That is an outrageous oversight that is simply inexcusable. That is the miscue, not the overthrow of the regime of one of our staunchest enemies. If taking down Saddam was such a bad idea, it should not have achieved the overwhelming support it did from the American politicians and people. Taking him out and then creating a power vacuum tailor made for a civil war was ill advised to say the least. No invasion should have even been considered until a realistic plan was firmly hashed out with several contingency scenarios. After we defeated the Iraqi conventional forces, several things should have been done immediately. First, the weapon stockpiles of the Iraqi military should have been secured and protected (as well as the many cultural treasures). The rampant looting of military equipment made an insurgency almost a foregone conclusion. Then, a sufficient ground force should have been deployed to provide security. Stabilizing the nation was an absolute must. When the Iraqi government collapsed, safety should have been immediately provided by an overwhelming number of coalition forces. It is certainly more difficult to "nation build" or even to just repair infrastructure with an active insurgency and a low grade civil war raging. Lastly, a workable interim or permanent government should have been immediately instituted. Certainly all this should have been done before any "mission accomplished" aircraft carrier photo opportunity.

Now, Iraq is a quagmire. The Coalition soldiers cannot pull out because it is obvious to everyone that a regional religious war would erupt with disastrous consequences. The politicians who advocate immediate withdrawal should have zero credibility in this debate. It is an inane position. A Middle Eastern war would devastate not only the region but also the world's oil supply. That certainly would not do the free market economies of the world any favors. It would also demolish any semblance of credibility for United States foreign policy. The only thing weaker than a tough guy who's scared to fight, is a tough guy who has been whipped by a weaker and smaller opponent. The U.S. plainly and simply cannot afford to reinforce its soft image. The chaos that would inevitably follow a coalition pullout would dwarf the nightmare that currently prevails in Iraq.

The division of Iraq into three separate nations has also been advocated as a possible solution for the situation. There would be several major negative results from such an action. It would severely strain the relationship between the United States and Turkey. The Turks adamantly oppose independence for the Kurds. An armed struggle between the two would be a distinct possibility. It could also very well lead to a general insurrection within eastern Turkey by the separatist minded Kurds. This could weaken the support for a secular Turkey and encourage the more radical Islamic elements there. The Shiite entity, if given independence, would be very much in danger of falling under the sway of Syria or Iran. Those two nations are staunch opponents of the U.S. and it would greatly prefer to isolate, rather than to empower them. The Sunni nation would be relatively small and weak and would need to come under the protection of its more powerful Sunni neighbors. A weak Sunni nation would also be very vulnerable to becoming a haven for al-Qaeda. A regional war could be ignited if the three new nations fight amongst themselves. Three small nations easily swayed by extremists or more powerful neighbors is not the way to proceed.

In summary, the Coalition cannot just "stay the course" in Iraq. What they are doing is not working and will never work. A true democracy will, in all likelihood, lead to a radical Shiite theocracy unable or unwilling to protect its minorities. A Coalition withdrawal would almost guarantee a regional bloodbath. They also cannot divide it into three weak easily influenced entities. A new approach must be employed.

Kurdish-inhabited area

Black Sea · GEORGIA
★ Tbilisi
Samsun
Ankara ★
Trabzon
ARMENIA
Yerevan ★
Baku ★
TURKMEN.
Balkanabat
Sivas
Erzincan
Erzurum
AZERBAIJAN
Caspian Sea
TURKEY
L. Tuz
Kayseri
Ardabil
Rasht
Konya
Malatya
L. Van
Van
Diyarbakir
Tabriz
Mersin
Adana
Gaziantep
Urmia
L. Urmia
Aras
Zanjan
Sari
Mediterranean
Aleppo
Mosul
Arbil
Sulaymaniyah
★ Tehran
CYPRUS
SYRIA
Kirkuk
Hamadan
IRAN
Qom
Sea Beirut
Homs
Euphrates
Tigris
Kermanshah
LEBANON ★
Damascus
Ramadi
Baghdad
Khorramabad
Haifa
3
IRAQ
Esfahan
ISRAEL
2
Karbala
Kut
Amarah
Jerusalem ★ Amman
Najaf
Ahvaz
Karun
1
Dead Sea
JORDAN
Nasiriyah
Basra
Shiraz
Suez
EGYPT
Aqaba
SAUDI ARABIA
Kuwait City ★
Bushehr
Tabuk
KUWAIT
Persian Gulf
Red Sea

Occupied by Israel:
1 - Gaza Strip
2 - West Bank
3 - Golan Heights

The Middle East

Chapter 5

There Is Nothing New Under The Sun

The current quagmire in Iraq is not a unique phenomenon. The British Empire faced an equally daunting dilemma after World War I. After the defeat of the decaying Ottoman Empire, the British were left occupying present day Israel, Jordan, Saudi Arabia, Iraq, and Egypt. All this territory had been under Turkish rule for centuries except for Egypt. It had been occupied by the British in 1882, but had remained under nominal Turkish control until it was officially annexed in 1914. Historically, a sultan in Constantinople (renamed Istanbul in 1930) ruled the Ottoman Empire. The sultan had been deposed prior to the Great War and the "Young Turks" had taken power. The Ottoman generals and the army now called the shots and when war came, they turned their backs on the British and French to side with the Kaiser's Germany. The Germans had trained much of the Ottoman officer corps and the Turks also could not resist a chance to fight their natural enemies, Tsarist Russia. Britain must have felt at least a tinge of remorse for supporting the Turks at the expense of the Russians in the previous decades. The Turks had recently intensified their efforts to exert more direct control over the remains of their empire. This did not lead to a widespread Arabic revolt, but it did increase their level of discontentedness. The British infamously landed at Gallipoli on the European side of the Dardanelle Straits in an effort to quickly take Constantinople. If successful this would have more than likely knocked the Turks out of the war in one fell swoop. However, the British, Australians, and New Zealanders were unable to break out of the landing zone. They inexplicably dawdled after they came ashore and allowed the Turks to rush troops to encircle the beachhead. The antagonists became locked in a nightmare battle of attrition. After horrendous casualties on both sides, the bridgehead was evacuated ignominiously. This did not by any means end the Turkish-British fighting. The British were desperate to protect the route to India, their most prized colonial territory. Sir Edmund Allenby was able to capture Jerusalem and another British force took Baghdad. They were aided by Arab guerilla fighters led by Sharif Feisal, the future king of Iraq. The quirky British officer, T.E. Lawrence, was also active with the Arabs; and he and Feisal formed a lifelong bond. The Arab irregulars were not overly effective against the professional Turkish soldiers in large-scale operations, but they tied down large numbers of troops with their hit and run tactics. When Allenby liberated Damascus, he allowed Feisal and his soldiers to ceremoniously enter the city first. Feisal quickly declared himself King of Syria. He was later forced from Syria by the French. They had received a mandate to govern there after the war from the League of Nations. After further losses, the Turks were forced to capitulate and sign the unfavorable Treaty of Sevres. Britain gained a mandate for most of the Middle East, excluding Syria and modern day Lebanon. Much like the modern day scenario, the victorious British did not have a workable plan in place to replace the Turkish governing institutions with cooperative ones. To provide security and quell the rebellions that were erupting, the British were forced to maintain a large and very expensive occupation force. This was an unacceptable long-term situation because they were still reeling from the huge expenditures and sacrifices of World War I. They also faced enormous pressure in Egypt for immediate independence and a general revolution in Ireland. To top it off, the resilient Turks were also a threat to the Kurdish region in Mesopotamia. Kemal Ataturk led the Turks at that time. He was the commanding general that ground out a victory for the Ottomans at Gallipoli. He would soon defeat the Greeks and drive them completely from Anatolia. He also found time to slaughter the Christian Armenians in his territories by the hundreds of thousands. The Turkish victories allowed them to scrap the Treaty of Sevres and renegotiate much more favorable terms. They were a very real threat to try to reconquer their lost possessions. The British could not leave a weak or unstable government in their mandates. Their situation eerily mirrored the Coalition's predicament in modern Iraq.

The British government led by David Lloyd George needed a workable solution fast to keep the region from spiraling out of control. Winston Churchill was given the task of reducing costs and trying to set up stable regional governments. True democracies were never considered because it would have obviously led to anti-British governments. They would also take a long time to imbed and this would not be cheap. Monarchies were deemed to be the most likely way to set up stable, friendly governments quickly. There were several candidates that could be considered for each region that would later become a nation. For Mesopotamia, which would become Iraq, T.E. Lawrence was a strong advocate for his old friend Feisal. Feisal was a strong candidate for several reasons. First of all, he was a member of the powerful Hashemite family of Arabia. They were descended from the clan of Muhammad through his daughter, Fatima and her husband, Ali. Being a direct descendant of Muhammad has always engendered a tremendous amount of respect in the Islamic world. The patriarch of the family at that time was King Hussein the Emir of Hijaz. This gave him control of Mecca, the most revered city of Islam. The Ottomans had favored the Hashemites, but they were strong advocates of a pan Arabic Empire. However, Feisal did have several rivals to the Mesopotamian throne. His older brother Abdullah was persuaded to forgo a claim on Iraq in exchange for becoming king of Transjordan. Jordan was seen as a lesser kingdom compared to Iraq. Churchill and Lawrence rightly or wrongly thought Feisal would be the better monarch. Another ferocious regional claimant was Abdul Aziz Al Saud. He had the backing of the fundamentalist Wahhabi sect of Sunnism. They were fierce warriors and were soon able to depose Hussein and his son Ali in the Hijaz and take over most of the Arabian Peninsula. Saud founded the Saudi Dynasty that still rules Saudi Arabia today. Perhaps if the British had foreseen the long-term effects of allowing a Wahhabi state, they would have supported Hussein more in his struggle against them. Osama Bin Laden is one of the more famous extremists to come from this movement. It was correctly surmised that Saud's interpretation of Islam would not be the best for a country made up more of Kurds and Shiites than Sunni Arabs. Local rulers were also exiled or subordinated to make way for Feisal. Churchill and his experts finally agreed at a conference in Cairo that Feisal would be king of Iraq. His inflexibility and obvious ambition were overlooked because of his prior service against the Turks and his impeccable Arab credentials. Churchill was convinced that installing Feisal was the cheapest and most expedient method of creating a functioning Iraqi government. The conference dignitaries and experts also drew up the modern day borders of the Middle East effectively creating Palestine, Transjordan, and Iraq. King Feisal did not turn out to be the pliant British puppet he was envisioned to be. He was, however, able to hold his new nation together. This was not a total victory for the British, but it created a working system of government and let them radically reduce their garrison and expenditures there. The Hashemite monarchy was overthrown in 1958. Iraq has remained a secular and viable nation under the rule of Sunni strongmen. It has weathered several wars, tribulations, and regime changes.

Chapter 6

You Don't Always Get What You Want

However grim things may appear in the region, there is definitely a historical precedent for an alternative, successful approach. The British created a stable government from a situation that was just as gloomy. They seriously considered an unequivocal pullout. However, this course of action was quickly rejected. They knew that they had an obligation to replace the system of government they had overthrown with something viable. The United States carries the same burden. History has not been kind to the nations who have abandoned wars and allies. Look at the well-deserved perception the world has of the French after they abandoned their colonial allies to the slaughter in Indochina and Algeria. The solution the British used in the 1920s would work just as well today.

A constitutional monarchy is the most promising option to extricate the United States and its allies from the mess they have created. It has the very real potential for a friendly, secular, united, and stable Iraqi government. This would also alleviate many of the obvious obstacles that a true democracy faces in Iraq. While it would not be a true democracy like the Bush administration had envisioned, it would be one of the most democratic governments in the Middle East, outside of Israel. This government would have a democratically elected parliament that would represent Iraq's constituent peoples. It would obviously have to imbue the king with more relative power than Western style constitutional monarchies, however.

He would have to be politically strong enough for his government to survive long-term. He would also need the power to prohibit extremist groups from participating in the government if they posed a risk to the nation's minority groups or the national security. The parliament would have to have input on domestic affairs and the distribution of the nation's tremendous oil wealth. A king would bring real stability to the reeling nation. Each election would no longer carry the tension of being perhaps a life or death decision for the losing parties. No matter who had the majority in the parliament, the Iraqi's could rely on the king to protect all his subjects, whether they are Sunni, Shiite, Christian, Arab, Kurd, or Turkoman. He could also ensure that the government stayed secular and did not fall into the hands of any one religious group. The Arabs and Kurds of today's Iraq still operate in a traditional clan based hierarchal system of power. A king is a concept that has ancient precedents and modern examples in their region. As a matter of fact, their neighboring Arab brethren in Jordan, Saudi Arabia, and Kuwait all have stable monarchies in place. It is a proven system in their culture in direct contrast to a republic. The controversial and contested election in 2000 between President Bush and Al Gore was heated enough in a nation that had a democratic tradition dating back two hundred and twenty-five years. A fledging Iraqi democracy could not conceivably survive that type of stress unless it had the security provided by an occupying force. Because the U.S. does not have the political will to be that force indefinitely, all solutions should be explored.

The key to making a constitutional monarchy work in Iraq would be the choice of a monarch. He could not be seen as a stooge of Washington as al-Maliki is perceived. He would have to be an Arab of influence with a history of leadership. He would need to have a preexisting strong base of support in the region. A weak king would not last long in power and would be widely susceptible to coups. However, he could not be too radical or despotic. It is my opinion that it would be absolutely necessary that he be a Sunni Arab for many reasons. The Sunnis have ruled Iraq for over five hundred years. They have proven that they can run the country. This is not to overlook their major blemishes in the human rights department, but it certainly is preferable to the current bloodbath we are seeing under Shiite control. The Shiites also have a dearth of secular leaders. The most influential of their people are clerics and an Iran style theocracy is certainly not what the Coalition soldiers are fighting and dying for. Even if a secular Shiite leader were found and installed, he would assuredly face a well-funded Sunni insurgency with the support of the surrounding Sunni nations. This would force him to ally strongly with Iran and Syria. That would not rank highly on Bush's diplomatic achievement list or his presidential legacy that he is so worried about. While a Sunni Arab monarch might not seem overly fair to the Shiites, there really is no plausible alternative. Since the U.S. foreign policy for Iraq has been plagued over the past few years with completely unrealistic goals with no hope of success, it is time to stop dealing in fantasy and start implementing workable solutions.

Far and away the most logical choice for a monarch in Iraq would be King Abdullah II of Jordan. His selection as king would have many favorable ramifications. It would instantly unite the countries of Jordan and Iraq. This would infuse the nation with over five and a half million Sunni Arabs. The Arabs in Iraq and the Arabs in Jordan are ethnically the same people. This would make the Sunni population in Iraq, Kurd and Arab, just slightly less than the Shiite population there. This demographic balancing act would alleviate the perception of the Shiites being grossly mistreated. King Abdullah II would actually be reestablishing the Hashemite monarchy in Iraq, which was overthrown in a bloody coup in 1958. He is the grandson of Abdullah I, whose brother Feisal ruled Iraq. He would instantly become a leader that the nation could rally around. Certainly the Sunni Arabs in Iraq would jump at the chance to restore their position of leadership. In the current Iraq policy, only the Kurds have a desire to see the al-Maliki government work. The Shiites are biding their time to replace al-Maliki with a cleric and the Sunni Arabs are fighting tooth and nail to prevent that from happening. An

70

Abdullah II kingdom would instantly mean that it was in the Sunnis vested interest to fall in line and support a stable government. Abdullah II would have to reach out to the Shiites and Kurds to prove that he could rule on their behalf as well. The fact that he can trace his family tree back to the clan of Muhammad himself certainly would help in this regard. The pan-Arabist movement is a dream that the Hashemites have always supported. The doctrine achieved tremendous popular support when it was made famous by Abdel Nasser. It would be a strong pull for Iraq's Shiites. They are Arabs just like the Sunni Arabs from Jordan and Iraq. Iranians are Persians, not Arabs. The pan-Arab proponents have always despaired that they were artificially separated by the great European colonial powers. The gravity of their ethnicity could help balance the centrifugal force of religious differences. The Shiite Arabs of Iraq for the most part fought bravely in the Iran-Iraq War and they have a long history within Iraq. Jordan was one of the few Arab countries that openly supported Iraq in their struggle with Iran. Jordan and Iraq have actually been united in the recent past. In 1958, they formed the Arab Federation. The union of the two Hashemite kingdoms was cut short when the coup overthrew the Iraqi monarchy. It only lasted approximately five months, but it proved that the two nations share a historical bond. A skillful policy by Abdullah II would need to reinforce the pan Arab ideal and make the Shiites feel comfortable. Certainly a secure nation, with religious freedom and a prosperous economy, would be very conducive to healing the wounds of the current strife. The city of Kirkuk would definitely need to be placed in the Kurdish region so that they would realize their days of being second rate Iraqis are over. In a stable environment with a strong and benevolent king, it is not unrealistic to envision the Kurds, Sunnis and Shiites living and working together again.

To see that happen would, first and foremost, require the end of the civil war that is being waged in the streets of Iraqi cities. A massive influx of Islamic peacekeepers would be necessary until the government and a national security force was in place. Obtaining these peacekeeping soldiers would not be hard. The Sunni neighbors of Iraq could be counted on to provide warriors in great numbers. The Turks understandably could not be involved due to sensibilities of the Kurds. The bulk of the peacekeepers would be projected to come from Egypt and Pakistan. Bosnia would also be expected to contribute soldiers after years of U.S. support and military training. Lebanon's military is notorious for its inability to go to war because of its factionalized state, but as a peacekeeping force it should be ideal. The alpha Arabs, the Saudis, would also be expected to help bankroll this force. The Saud royal family may not be ecstatic to see their old Hashemite rivals in power in Iraq, but they would greatly prefer this to a Shiite state or to a raging civil war there. As the Islamic peacekeepers arrived and spread out, the coalition forces would ideally exit the country. Initially, U.S. and British forces could withdraw to the Iranian and Syrian borders to prevent weapons smuggling, border crossing insurgents, or a full-scale invasion. A rapid reaction force near Baghdad may also be considered until the situation stabilizes. Once a stable government is in place, all Coalition troops should be completely withdrawn. Carrier groups in the Mediterranean Sea and Persian Gulf could react quickly enough if the situation deteriorated again. Realistically, the U.S. and British could have their troops completely withdrawn in three to six months. A huge factor in this timeline would be the new combined Jordanian-Iraqi Army. This would obviously have at its base the current army of Jordan and the former Republican Guard of Iraq's old army. Iraq's old officers and soldiers have not forgotten how to fight. However, they have no interest in sticking their necks out for a failed regime. They would never lend their support to the current U.S. pipedream. Jordan's military has actually been known as the Arab Legion since its inception, showing Jordan's support of a united Arab people. A motivated and professional army could be molded into being within a matter of months.

The biggest obstacle for the success of this plan is actually convincing Abdullah II to accept the risk of merging the two nations and becoming their monarch. He knows the history of the region well and the 1958 coup would have to make him somewhat apprehensive of a combined throne. However, I believe he would accept the challenge after careful deliberation. Today Jordan is a small, relatively poor nation that fears its neighbors. A combined Jordan-Iraq, or modern day Arab Federation, would be a regional super power. It would have a large economy, population, and army. The oil deposits in Iraq alone make it a very attractive kingdom. His old kingdom of Jordan had relatively few natural resources. Ruling from Baghdad would also be a powerful temptation for any Arab leader. For centuries the city has been one of the most important centers of power in the Arab world. As a true Hashemite, Abdullah II could really not pass up this opportunity. A combined Jordan-Iraq would be the pan Arab powerhouse that the prestigious family has long clamored for and dreamed of leading. He would need several security guarantees for at least five years. If Iran or Syria invaded his kingdom, the U.S. would have to be willing to intervene. The Jordan-Iraq military would soon become more powerful than either of those nations, so the security arrangement would not have to be long term. Abdullah II would also have to have assurance that if the plan failed, he could abdicate the Iraqi throne and still retain his Jordanian kingdom.

With regards to Iraq's neighbors, this plan would have several benefits. A combined Jordan-Iraq would instantly become a leader in the Arab world. Their secular approach to government would be in stark contrast to the support of Wahhabism exhibited by the Saudis. Israel and Jordan already have a preexisting peace treaty. This is very controversial in the Arab world, but the normalization of relations between Iraq and Israel would be beneficial to the stability of the entire region. Combining Jordan and Iraq would also open a window of opportunity to solve the Palestinian-Israeli impasse. Israel and the West Bank were formerly part of Transjordan. It is true that Jordan renounced the right to the West Bank on July 30, 1988 after a prolonged struggle with the PLO and pressure from other Arab regimes. However, with the combined resources of Jordan and Iraq, the West Bank territory outside of

Israel's security fence could be ceded directly to Jordan-Iraq. This would give Israel a stable peace partner and allow Fatah and Hamas to be bypassed. The Palestinian Arabs have not shown even the slightest ability to govern themselves without corruption, extremism, infighting, or belligerence toward Israel. If they were once again united with Jordan and represented in the Jordan-Iraq parliament, they could again become proud Arab citizens of a powerful nation. This would be in direct contrast to the currently forlorn, destitute Palestinian refugees dependant on the benevolence of other Arabs. They could stop perceiving themselves as victims without a home and focus on their economy and culture. This would also add over two million Sunni Arabs to Jordan-Iraq and make Sunnism demographically the most practiced version of Islam there. Fatah and Hamas have proven to be incapable of forming a viable, responsible state for the Palestinians in the West Bank or the Gaza Strip. Abdullah II of Jordan does not currently have the resources or power to incorporate the West Bank back into the Jordanian fold. Abdullah II of a combined Jordan-Iraq could easily manage the undertaking, even in the face of Syrian, Fatah, Hamas, and Saudi opposition. With the West Bank, Jordan, and Iraq combined to form a moderate Arab superpower, Gaza could logically be ceded to Egypt. The Egyptians can provide security there and prevent Hamas from attacking into Israel. Both the Gaza Palestinians and Israelis have recently advocated tying the Gaza economy to Egypt, not Israel. Hamas would slowly lose influence and power there as living conditions for the Palestinians improved and their isolation ended. Similarly, the Palestinian refugees camped in Lebanon could be brought into the nation. This would certainly alleviate a major headache for the Lebanese. As the Hashemite Kingdom of Jordan-Iraq's influence rose, the influence of Syria's would fall. If the American State Department was willing, it could use that opportunity to further isolate the Syrian dictatorship. A policy that rewarded the friends of America and punished its enemies could very well end the malevolent tendencies of the Syrians. The Golan Heights should be formally recognized as Israeli. This would be a severe blow to the Syrians and a deserved reward for Israel's release of any claim over Gaza or the West Bank (after negotiations for a mutually agreed upon border). An autonomous Kurdish region with a no fly zone should be set up over the Kurdish region of Syria. This would not only further reduce Syria's prestige, but it could lead to Syria's Kurdish region uniting with Jordan-Iraq's Kurdistan. Syria's Kurds could be "allowed" to hold a referendum to join their Kurdish brothers in Jordan-Iraq, further cementing the Kurds' loyalty to the nation. Even though they have been severely mistreated in the past within Iraq, with regional autonomy and national good will, the Kurds would be an invaluable asset to their country. The rulers of Syria are Alawite Shiites and currently represent only around sixteen percent of the Syrian population. With the majority of their nation being Sunnis, they are in a more precarious situation than many outsiders realize. The Syrians should no longer be allowed to obstruct U.S. policy in the region or terrorize the Lebanese. If they lost the Golan Heights and their Kurdish region, they would be severely diminished in power at the same time that Jordan-Iraq's power would be increasing. Iran would find a Jordan-Iraq powerhouse to be a westward bulwark against their extremism. Their funding of Hizbollah and Hamas could be curtailed and rendered irrelevant. If the Shiites of Iraq-Jordan are allowed religious freedom and buy into a pan-Arab vision for the future, Iran would lose their breeding ground for meddling in Iraqi affairs. Turkey would not be overly pleased to have a strong Jordan-Iraq that could protect the Kurds. Certainly, they would rattle their swords at adding Syrian Kurdish lands to the nation. However, Turkey is long overdue in addressing their horrific human rights record. The Kurds in Turkey are humans. They deserve to preserve their culture, teach their children, speak their language, and worship as they see fit. If the Americans and British will not stand up for the Kurds, perhaps Abdullah II will. His combined nation certainly would have the power to stop the Turks from their frequent punitive incursions into Iraq.

Hopefully, the Bush administration and their allies will seriously consider a Hashemite constitutional monarchy ruling over Jordan, Iraq, and the Palestinian West Bank. It would achieve all of their stated goals for Iraq and pull a victory out of the jaws of defeat. I believe that it would not only be very realistic to implement quickly, but also have several auxiliary benefits to the region and the world.

Map of Proposed Arab Federation

Part Three
The Transcaucasus

Chapter 7

A Genocide By Any Other Name

   The impasse between the former Soviet republics of
Azerbaijan and Armenia would be shockingly simple to solve.
It is embarrassing that the United States, Great Britain, France,
and Russia do not have the cumulative resolve to stand up for
justice in this case. After a very brief history of the events and
peoples that are involved, the honorable course of action that
should be pursued immediately will be discussed.
   The Armenian Kingdom was established in the
Transcaucasus region by 300 B.C. It reached its greatest extent
under King Tigranes II (Tigranes the Great). Under his rule,
the Armenians stretched from the Mediterranean to the Caspian
Sea. The missionary work of Saint Gregory the Illuminator
helped to convert the Armenians to Christianity around 300
A.D. They follow an eastern form of Orthodoxy. The
Armenians were located in a natural gateway for invading
armies from both the east and the west. They have
consequently endured countless invasions over the millennia.
Armenia was divided between the Persians and the Eastern
Roman Empire in the 380s. The Persians dissolved the
Kingdom of Armenia in their areas of control, replacing the
king with an appointed governor in 428. This is the time
period that the area that is now known as Nagorno-Karabagh
(then known as Artsakh and Utik) was separated from
Armenia. It was included in the Caucasian Albanian province
of the Sassinid Empire. In the 630s the Transcaucasus was
invaded and conquered by the Arabs. The

Armenians slowly gained more autonomy as the Arab power declined and in the 880s an independent Armenia reemerged along with several smaller Armenian principalities. In 1045 the Byzantine Empire conquered the Armenians but their rule was not to last long. The Seljuk Turks defeated the Byzantines at the battle of Mantzikert in 1071. By 1075, the Turks controlled all of Armenia. As Seljuk power waned, Armenian influence again reemerged, but the region was soon to be ravaged by wave after wave of brutal eastern invaders. The Mongols conquered and devastated the whole region in the 1200s A.D. When the Mongol empire fragmented, they again laid it waste vying for its control. The Turkmen under Tamerlane took control in the late 1300s. As successive Turkish groups tried to establish their power, the land and people were racked by disease, famine, and wholesale massacres. The mountainous region of Nagorno-Karabagh allowed the Armenians there to retreat upward and maintain the Armenian culture. Fortunately, the region was fertile enough for the people to be self-sufficient. In the 1500s, the Ottoman Turks and the Persians battled for domination predictably causing much hardship and a new wave of devastation. The Persians destroyed anything that could be used by the Ottomans and deported thousands of the area's inhabitants thus creating a wasteland. Armenia was effectively divided between the Turks and the Safavid Persian Empire. The next big shake up in the area occurred when Tsarist Russia conquered the eastern Armenian lands in the early 1800s. The unfortunate, western part remained in the Ottoman Empire. The Ottomans massacred the Armenians there in the tens of thousands during the late 1890s. It was during this time that pan-Turkism began to emerge in popularity among the Turks. This was also the time period when the word Azerbaijani is first used to describe the Turks of the eastern Transcaucasus. The Azeris follow Shiite Islam, while the Turks of the Ottoman Empire follow Sunni Islam. Previously, they had been known as Tatars. The Turks envisioned a Turkish powerhouse that stretched from Eastern Europe to Central Asia. The only thing geographically stopping this from being a reality was the

Armenian people. They would soon pay a terrible price for this. The Great War saw the Ottoman Empire join Germany and the Austria-Hungarian Empire in their fight against the Russians, British, and French. A Turkish thrust towards Baku was stopped by the Russians at the Battle of Sarikamis. If the Turks had captured Baku, it would have united the Turks of the Ottoman Empire with the Turks of Azerbaijan. Now the fury of the Ottomans was turned in full force on the Armenians. There were the usual massacres, but there was also a state supported "deportation" effort that rounded up the Armenians and sent them to concentration camps. The Armenians were not provided with food or medicine during the process. They also suffered beatings, rapes, and systematic murder. Very few Armenians were actually "lucky" enough to be deported. The vast majority suffered the indignity of being slaughtered or starved to death because of their religion, their ethnicity and their location. Between five hundred thousand and one and a half million Armenians perished during World War I at the hands of the Turks. The initial Russian success in the region was turned on its head after the Russian October Revolution in 1918. The prewar population of Armenians in the Ottoman Empire that numbered around two million no longer existed. The Turks now turned their attention to the Armenians that were under Russian rule. With the Russian Army disintegrating, the Armenians took over their own defense. Their most famous leader was the warrior Andranik. They declared independence from Russia on May 28, 1918; one day after Azerbaijan had done likewise. Without any hope of Russian assistance and with hostile Turks on either side, the Armenian Republic signed the very unfavorable Treaty of Batum. This agreement ceded western Armenia to Turkey. The Turks had been forced by the victors of World War 1 to sign the Treaty of Sevres, which had promised an independent Armenia under the protection of the United States. With the failure of the League of Nations Treaty in the U.S., all hope of American protection evaporated and the Turks could act without restraint. The British began a northward movement out of Iran and into the Transcaucasus. They hoped to fill the void left by the Russians and possibly assist the White Russian Armies fighting the Bolsheviks. The British Empire at the time contained massive numbers of Muslims. It had incorporated India, Egypt, Mesopotamia and Palestine over the preceding years. Its officer corps was used to Islamic conscripts and generally had warm feelings towards them. The Armenians hoped the British would remain impartial and provide protection from the Azeri Turks. These aspirations were quickly dashed as the British stood by and allowed the Azerbaijanis to begin systematic ethnic cleansing programs. Heroic resistance by the Armenians in Nagorno-Karabagh staved off Turkish armies bent on annihilation. Unable to conquer the mountainous region and unable to force it to accept Azerbaijani rule, the Azeris turned to siege tactics. All trade with Armenians in Nagorno-Karabagh was outlawed. The British withdrew from the Transcaucasus in 1919, leaving the Armenians in the midst of an artificial famine to their fate. The British presence had stopped the Turks from invading from the west, but it only intensified the mistreatment of the Armenians by the Azerbaijanis. As the British withdrew, an ominous mutual assistance pact was signed between the new Turkish government and the Azerbaijanis. In August of 1920, a resurgent Red Army was able to move into Georgia, Armenia, and Azerbaijan, while the complicit Turkish army stormed in from the west. The Turks forced the Armenians to sign the Treaty of Alexandropol, which basically confirmed the borders set by the Baku Treaty and denied the right of an independent Armenia to be protected by the U.S. In 1921, the Treaty of Kars replaced the Alexandropol treaty. Russia ceded Armenian Kars and the Armenian region around Mount Ararat to the Turks. In an effort to secure peace with the Turks, Lenin was more than willing to give up Armenian territory. The treaty also stipulated that the Nakhichevan Region would be separated from Armenia and given to Soviet Azerbaijan. To add insult to injury, on July 5, 1921, the Azerbaijanis received Nagorno-Karabagh because of its "economic ties" to Azerbaijan. It is amusing that the years of outright blockade and forced famine could be referred to as "economic ties." The population of Nagorno-Karabagh at the time it was awarded to the Azerbaijan S.S.R. was roughly 94% Armenian. This number is amazing considering the years of massacres, starvation, and invasions that had preceded its transfer. Constant unrest in the region resulted in it receiving special autonomous status in 1923. The Azerbaijanis systematically ethnically cleansed the Lachin area between the Armenian S.S.R. and Nagorno-Karabagh. They also removed the northern regions of Nagorno-Karabagh from the autonomous region even though they clearly had an overwhelming Armenian majority. These lands are still claimed by today's defacto independent Nagorno-Karabagh, but they are occupied firmly by the Azerbaijanis and have been emptied of Armenians. The Armenians in Nagorno-Karabagh faced rampant discrimination under Soviet rule and large numbers of them emigrated from the region. At the same time Azerbaijani Turks were encouraged to move in to strengthen their claim on the area. By 1979, the Armenian population represented only around 76% of Nagorno-Karabagh. During these Soviet years every time the national leadership changed, petitions were sent to Moscow to combine Nagorno-Karabagh with Armenia to no avail. Right up until the breakup of the Soviet Union, Armenian villagers were often forced to leave Azerbaijan. In February 1988, against the backdrop of Gorbachev's glasnost policies and massive demonstrations in Armenia for the return of her lost territory, a massacre of Armenians in the Azeri capital of Baku took place. After Gorbachev dismissed all possibilities of border modifications, the Karabagh Soviet declared independence from Azerbaijan and unification with Armenia. As the Soviet Union fell apart, its armies left or sold huge amounts of munitions to both sides. The independence of Azerbaijan and Armenia on December 31, 1991, cleared the way for open hostilities. Early victories by the Armenians gained them the Lachin strip, the land bridge between Armenia and its lost areas of Nagorno-Karabagh. These victories toppled the Azerbaijani government and its new leader looked to Turkey more than Russia for an ally. The Azeris launched a large offensive that threatened to overrun the Armenians of

Nagorno-Karabagh, but it was halted and a counteroffensive initiated that soon reclaimed the lost territory. Both Armenia and Azerbaijan used the war as a cover to empty itself of its opposing minority. Atrocities occurred in both nations as each side struggled for supremacy. An Armenian offensive in 1993 seized the Azeri city of Kelbajar. Turkey and Pakistan then cosponsored United Nations Resolution 822, which passed in the U.N. Security Council. It affirmed that Nagorno-Karabagh was part of Azerbaijan and called for the Armenians to withdraw from Kelbajar. Now the Armenians pressed their advantage and were able to seize large chunks of Azerbaijan. Early 1994 again saw an initially successful Azeri invasion. Like its previous invasions, it was ultimately stopped with great loss of life and its gains partially reversed. Several Azerbaijani governments came and went in an effort to find victorious leadership. At one point Turkey sent troops to the Armenian border and looked likely to intervene, but warnings from Russia kept them at bay. On May 16, 1994, a cease-fire was signed and a stalemate has ensued since that time. The de facto independent Republic of Nagorno-Karabagh occupies nine percent of Azerbaijan's territory. This figure excludes Nagorno-Karabagh itself. The Republic of Armenia has not had the political power to unite with their brethren. They fear the repercussions from the Turks and Azeris. Turkey and Azerbaijan have maintained blockades of both Armenian entities. No nation, not even Armenia, currently recognizes the independence of Nagorno-Karabagh. Azerbaijan has made repeated threats to once again explore a military solution and all negotiating efforts have failed.

The Transcaucasus

Chapter 8

Live By The Sword

     The United States, like every other nation of the world, refuses to acknowledge Nagorno-Karabagh's independence. All negotiations between the belligerents break down when only autonomy within Azerbaijan is offered as an option for the Armenians in the disputed region. So as the economies of Armenia and Nagorno-Karabagh crumble under a Turkish/Azeri embargo, Azerbaijan is training and equipping its military with proceeds from its massive oil deposits. The situation may appear to be in limbo, but disaster looms on the horizon.

     As the leader of the western world, the United States should immediately and unequivocally recognize the independence of Nagorno-Karabagh and allow it to unite with Armenia. Negotiations should be held to resolve territorial issues, but the Lachin corridor would have to stay under Armenian control. If the Armenians and Azeris both agreed, the northern part of Nagorno-Karabagh under Azeri control could be exchanged for Azeri territory under Armenian control. Because all areas behind the front lines of both sides have been ethnically cleansed, it makes more sense to recognize the current areas of control as national borders. The U.S. should then help Armenia with a substantial financial aid package to jumpstart its frozen economy. Many pundits will claim this is entirely unfair. I would concur wholeheartedly. Any fair resolution would require an indemnity and territorial compensation from Turkey to Armenia. Turkish concessions are not a realistic possibility, but to say that Armenians don't deserve to be able to protect themselves in their own nation is laughable. The Turks tried to wipe the Armenians off the face of the Earth. Even after the genocide of the 1910s concluded, the area of western Armenia ceded to the Turks from the Russians was cleansed. To this day the Turks deny that the genocide took place. The State Department of the United States is also hesitant to confirm it for fear of upsetting their Turkish Allies. When the U.S. Congress recently was on the verge of acknowledging that the genocide did indeed occur, our Turkish "allies" threatened to recall their ambassador. President Bush was quick to sooth their fears and Congress let the matter drop. Adolph Hitler drew inspiration from the Turks when he proposed a similar "solution" for the Jews. He casually noted that nobody speaks of the annihilation of the Armenians. The unwise policy of placating the Turks has gone on far too long. It is true that they served a strategic purpose in the Cold War against the Russians. It is also true, that as a secular Islamic power, they can help combat radical Islam. However, the price the world has paid for such appeasement policies has been appallingly high. The Turks not only massacred the Armenians, but also 1,300,000 Greeks were brutally expelled from Turkish Anatolia at the conclusion of the Greek-Turk War following World War 1. The Greeks were certainly not without blame, but their presence there was over three thousand years old and far predated the Turkish arrival. The Turks continue to treat the Kurds as second-class citizens and use overwhelming force and martial law to keep them in line. Using NATO weaponry, the Turks launched an invasion of Cyprus, almost starting another Greek-Turk war. They currently maintain a military occupation of over a third of Cyprus. The U.S. has not been rewarded for their embarrassing, unwavering support of the Turks. The Turkish government blocked American plans to invade northern Iraq with ground troops that would have had to pass through Turkey. They are constantly threatening to invade northern Iraq to attack the Kurds. They have conducted bombing raids against the Kurds in Iraq. This pattern of behavior is unacceptable, but they refuse to heed U.S. calls for restraint. It is embarrassing for the leading democratic nations to continue to walk on eggshells around the Turks. What if they stopped encouraging this abysmal behavior and held them to the same standard to which other nations are being held? If the Turks truly want to be an ally to the U.S. and a responsible member of NATO, then they should be able to conform to the same standard as the other members. If they insist on continuing their centuries old practice of being a regional bully, then NATO should not facilitate and subsidize this practice. If Germany started an economic blockade of Israel, they would be widely condemned. The Turks should also be forced to, once and for all, leave the Armenians in peace. The Azerbaijan claims to Nagorno-Karabagh have always been based on their desire to conquer it, not on any historical claim they have to the land. The Azeris have completely cleansed the Nakhichevan region of its sizable Armenian component. Few Armenians have little doubt what would ensue if their armies were defeated by either of the surrounding Turkish nations. That is why Armenia timidly refuses to even acknowledge Nagorno-Karabagh's obvious independence. The Turkish military is far and away more powerful than the combined forces of the Armenians. With their unbroken history of aggression, this threat is a terrifying prospect to the Armenians. The United States and Great Britain should take the only honorable position and let the Armenians unite in a contiguous nation. I realize that the Azerbaijani's possess tremendous oil resources, and that the Turks are NATO allies. However, it is unconscionable to abandon the Armenians once again to their fate. Sometimes responsible nations have to do what is right and not what is easy or economically advantageous. The Russians would certainly be an obstacle to resolving the standoff. While it would appear that they would stand up for their allies in Armenia, they have actually utilized the stalemate to keep troops posted in the region and maintain their influence there. Skilled U.S. diplomacy should be able to easily overcome their objections. If nothing else worked, certainly the Russians would be more inclined to help if they were allowed to annex Belarus and the Russian populated regions of the Crimea. The old U.S. Cold Warriors have wasted a lot of leverage and potential diplomatic breakthroughs by stubbornly continuing to thwart the Russians instead of working with them. With the Russians on board, Armenia, Nagorno-Karabagh and the Lachin strip could become a unified entity. For decades, the Turks have taken land from the Armenians. They have driven them from their homes or slaughtered them by the thousands. The world powers have callously and consistently turned a blind eye to the situation. A change in American policy is long overdue. The areas of control as they stand today should be recognized as the new national boundaries of Armenia. The ghosts of millions of slaughtered Armenians might then be able to rest in peace.

Conclusion

      United States foreign policy in the Balkans, Middle East, and the Transcaucasus needs a major overhaul. The current courses of action are extremely partial, naïve, and hypocritical. While claiming no anti-Serb bias in the former Yugoslavia, the U.S. has orchestrated policies to ensure the Serbs lost three conflicts. A blind eye was turned to the modernization of the Croatian Army and its ethnic cleansing of the Croatian (Krajina) Serbs. In Bosnia U.S. air power intervened directly to help alter the balance in favor of the Bosniaks and Bosnian Croats. In Kosovo, a conflict dating back over 600 years, air power was again used to drive the Serb military and police out. To top it all off, no measure was taken to protect the Serb civilians there, so the were brutally ethnically cleansed from their ancient heartland. Without even a hint of remorse, the U.S. then decided to unilaterally declare Kosovo independent. This essentially handed the disputed region to the Albanians, who were never remotely pressured to compromise in any fashion. Because Bosnia was left in dual state that has no chance of viability after peacekeepers leave, expensive international forces keep the adversaries apart. Croatia has not been forced to allow the Krajina Serbs to return to their homes or in compensation turn over Serb populated regions in Bosnia. Kosovo will require peacekeepers just to prevent the Albanians from finishing off the few remaining

Serb enclaves. Clearly an international Balkan peace conference with each antagonist treated fairly would be a welcome departure from the current "we will bomb and rearm until the Serbs lose" policy. Allowing the Serb populated parts of Kosovo and Bosnia to unite with Serbia would allow international forces to be withdrawn. If the territorial settlements were fair it would alleviate the need for the future Balkan wars that now seem inevitable.

In Iraq, the U.S. is trying to force feed democracy on an unwilling civilization that predates it by millennia. No matter how many "milestones" the occupation force achieves, the second they pull out the Iraqi government will crumble. The Sunnis will rise in rebellion, the Kurds will secede, and the Shiites will replace the secular government with a theocracy. The billions upon billions of dollars spent on this nation-building pipe dream will disappear in the Iraqi sand and blood. It seems far more logical to try a strategy that has proved successful in past in Iraq. A constitutional monarchy would give the nation a strong leader, some democratic aspects, and at least a chance of survival. If Jordan, the West Bank, and Iraq were combined under King Abdullah II, the Arab peoples of those countries will be united in a powerhouse nation. The Palestinians can break out of their perpetual victim stereotype that has served them so poorly and become a functioning society again. The Arabs have not forgotten that they are one people divided artificially by the Western colonial powers. They speak the same language and share the same culture. Rather than impose the American system on them for a few futile years, I contend it would be better to give them what they want; a stable, strong government that allows for security, prosperity, and prestige. They would then have the strength to combat radicalism and could help keep the Syrians and Iranians in line. We have been led to believe that staying the course and utter defeat are the only two options. I hope that I have made a case that there is a third option that has a high chance for success.

The American policy regarding Nagorno-Karabagh and the Armenians in general is embarrassing. The Azerbaijani

Turks have never constituted the majority of the population in Nagorno-Karabagh. This is despite their attempts at ethnic cleansing, starvation, and settlement. U.S. politicians deride the Iranian leadership for questioning the holocaust, but refuse to take a stand against the Turkish denial of the genocide of their Armenian population. It is time to stop making excuses for and placating the Turks. The independence of Nagorno-Karabagh should be recognized without further delay. It should also be allowed to unite with Armenia. The economic problems are severe and have been exacerbated tremendously by the Turk/Azeri blockade. Providing substantial economic assistance would be beneficial and the moral thing to do.

The conflicts discussed in this book have deep historical causes. Understanding these issues can change the outlook of American foreign policy. It is a reasonable hope that instead of hoping for expensive stalemates, we can begin looking for real solutions.

Notes

1. Tim Judah, *Kosovo: War and Revenge* (New Haven: Yale University Press, 2000), p. 53.

2. Tim Judah, *Kosovo: War and Revenge* (New Haven: Yale University Press, 2000), p. 184.

3. John Heilprin, "UN Security Council Meets on Kosovo" (Associated Press, 17 Feb.2008).

Selected Bibliography

Books

Burg, Steven L. and Shoup, Paul S. *The War In Bosnia-Herzegovina: Ethnic Conflict and International Intervention* (Armonk: M.E. Sharpe, 1999).

Catherwood, Christopher. *Churchill's Folly: How Winston Churchill Created Modern Iraq* (New York: Carroll & Graf, 2004).

Chorbajian, Levon, Patrick Donabedian and Claude Mutafian. *The Caucasian Knot: The History and Geo-Politics of Nagorno-Karabagh* (Atlantic Highlands: Zed Books, 1994).

Judah, Tim. *The Serbs: History, Myth and the Destruction of Yugoslavia* (New Haven: Yale University Press, 1997).

Judah, Tim. *Kosovo: War and Revenge* (New Haven: Yale University Press, 2000).

O'Shea, Brendon. *Crisis At Bihac: Bosnia's Bloody Battlefield* (Phoenix Mill: Sutton, 1998).

Salabi, Kamal. *The Modern History of Jordan* (New York: I.B. Tauris, 1998).

Shrader, Charles R. *The Muslim-Croat Civil War in Central Bosnia: A Military History, 1992-1994* (College Station: Texas A & M University Press, 2003).

Thomas, N. and Mikulan, K. *The Yugoslav Wars (1): Slovenia & Croatia 1991-95* (New York: Osprey, 2006).

Thomas, N. and Mikulan, K. *The Yugoslav Wars (2): Bosnia, Kosovo, and Macedonia 1992-2001* (New York: Osprey, 2006).

Magazine Articles and News Services

Mackey, Robert R. "Policing the Empire: How the Royal Air Force won its wings in the Middle East." Military History 24:5 July/August 2007: 26-35.

Heilprin, John. "UN Security Council Meets on Kosovo." Associated Press. 17 Feb. 2008.